THE ENGLISH GARDEN ROOM

EDITED BY ELIZABETH DICKSON

PHOTOGRAPHS BY FRITZ VON DER SCHULENBURG

WEIDENFELD AND NICOLSON
LONDON

ACKNOWLEDGEMENTS

I HAVE BEEN INTERESTED in conservatories since childhood in Scotland when my Scottish grandmother used to take us on brisk trots to The Botanic Gardens within walking distance of our house in Edinburgh. The glass buildings there would appear to us like beautiful icebergs, glacial edifices, spiky and strange, which beckoned as a prize place to sit in or explore after our expeditions along paths flanked by holly and rhododendrons. The impression of these places as perceived by a six-year-old once inside was one of plants with curious shapes and colours, an atmosphere damp, warm and exotic. All of this was in contrast to the northern climate I was brought up in, whether in the city or on the beaches of East Lothian where we walked in school crocodile.

About nine years ago I found myself in the conservatory at Chatsworth where the combination of elegant glass and ironwork, plant forms, water and a mysterious fusion of scents once again provoked the imagination and I came to realize that what has been described as 'the eternal stillness' of these glass chambers is, for me, the clue to their fascination. Conservatories have different meanings to different people but I enjoy the romantic notion that they were built by the Victorians as ferny places where people could escape to and where daughters would receive and accept proposals of marriage.

I owe special gratitude to Michael Dover, my Editor at Weidenfeld for his belief in the idea and for his help and advice in putting the book together, to Simon Bell for his design and to Penny Clarke for her assiduous editing.

Many people, friends and colleagues have also helped me. I would like to give a special mention to Joyce Dickson, Anthony Lord, Jessica Jessel, Cathryn Cawdor, Emma Marrian, Carol and Alistair Gavin, Camilla Fairbairn, Terence Rodrigues, Julian Barrow, Laura Blond, Belinda Montagu, Ivry Freyberg, Maureen Cleave, Pat White, Frances Pemberton, Nicholas Johnston, Christopher Gibbs, Robin Hanbury-Tenison, Valentine Fleming, Martin Drury of the National Trust and to The Chelsea Gardener for the kind loan of plants for photography.

I would like to set down here my gratitude and admiration for photographer Fritz von der Schulenburg and his assistant Karen Howes for their enthusiasm and skill; to my son Alexander and daughter Catherine for their encouragement and to Caroline Brakspear, my assistant and researcher whose patience and humour has once again been vital in transforming an idea into a finished book.

Elizabeth Dickson
London 1986

Designed by Simon Bell

George Weidenfeld & Nicolson Limited
91 Clapham High Street
London SW4 7TA

ISBN 0 297 79006 4

Filmset by Keyspools Ltd, Golborne, Lancashire
Colour separations by Newsele Litho Ltd
Printed and bound in Italy by L.E.G.O. Vicenza

(HALF TITLE PAGE) *Christopher McLaren and his children in the glasshouse which is entered through double sliding doors. The George III wood and cane-back garden chairs are from Bodnant and painted to simulate bamboo; the floor matting comes from Habitat, and the printed material is by Warners.*

(FRONTISPIECE) *Busts from antiquity form the silent guardians of the orangery at Port Eliot. The newly restored seat has graced the garden for over a hundred years.*

CONTENTS

FOREWORD

WHAT *is* a garden room? Historically a walled garden adjoining the house was a 'room without a roof', and so might be termed a garden room. But Miss Dickson's twenty-five garden rooms all have roofs, and apart from a garden room on wheels, a room with a window, a temple, a grotto and oddments, all come under the title of conservatory. How mundane is this word 'conservatory'; how ingenious of Clough Williams-Ellis to rename it 'crystal room', and how delightfully this book carries the reader into the magic world that lies within! For in this technocratic age it is the magic that matters and not the size, structure or convenience, however pressing these may be. So let us follow the author's explanations into the emotions and feelings of as great a variety of personalities as you are likely to meet in the complex society of this day and age.

First, however, we must approach her inner world through her outer landscape. There is the old Tuscan temple imported by lorry and rebuilt stone by stone, to bring a sense of historic time into a romantic landscape; nostalgic, but beyond the reach of Everyman. We can enjoy at a distance, too, Clough's exciting concepts at Maenan which included a proposed obelisk as a flue to scatter Lady Aberconway's ashes. There are many landscape delights such as these, but we must hasten on to that which is of concern to us all, the universal conservatory itself. Yet we must pause once more, for it is impossible to pass the great Victorian glass houses without a sigh for things long past. One reads nostalgically Lord Harrowby's description of the winter ritual of

Sunday tea in the conservatory: 'My mother and the other ladies dressed for it as if they were in the tropics, in long spotted muslins with flowing ribbons'. And how well does Lady Newborough summarize the ending of an era:

> The stable clock strikes half-past three
> Gone are the staff that brought us tea.

In these essays we experience a world long past – its dignity and grandeur recalling the words of the historian G.M.Trevelyan: 'the world is not likely to see again so fine and broad a culture for many centuries to come'.

The first question that arises, is 'what is a garden room, conservatory, glass house *for*?' Horticulturally, of course, to grow plants which could not otherwise have lived and secondarily to give compulsive pleasure to the humans who tend them. There are side-lines by which the conservatory became a dining or a tea room with plants as decor. There could even be no plants at all: David Mlinaric argues logically enough that garden rooms are built *by* humans *for* humans. These are exceptions and the supreme purpose is the creation of a crystal box that for a brief period carries you to the shores of the Mediterranean (or some equally warm area) to which we are biologically attracted. So now let us follow Elizabeth Dickson not only into the magic box itself, but into the minds of those who created it out of the subconscious.

Each description of the crystal room by the several authors is individual to his or her self. Each

conveys the impact of exotic natural form upon the emotions. Of the many vivid descriptions I have chosen that by John Merton.

At nine o'clock this Sunday, 26 January 1986, I opened the curtains. A low sun was lighting up brilliantly fifteen Eucharist lily flowers within three feet of the window. The drooping heads were four feet high and, sitting on the carpet, I could look up at the beautiful rarely seen green structures inside the lily.

He adds that he rushed off to get a camera, but this is an anti-climax for only the mind can perpetuate the intangible moment; the photograph will confuse the image.

In the study of human nature alone this book is both a pleasure and an instruction to read. As an exploration into present needs rather than past triumphs it tells a story of immeasurable importance. The crystal box may or may not be distinguished architecturally, but it is the union of this with what lies within that is magic, and this magic, on whatever scale you like (for magic has no scale), is accessible to every family of the welfare state who is above the bread line and does not live in a tower block. I do not think it is fully realized in a modern society that while we derive our overwhelming technocracy from the cosmos, we derive our bodies and most of our deep subconscious from mother earth. Our love of flowers (as well as trees) derives from the forest life of many thousands of years ago. We subconsciously still yearn for their companionship, their gaiety as part of the cycle of nature. It is because I feel Elizabeth Dickson has pointed a way to release frustrations in our everyday lives that I find her book not only fascinating fireside reading but one of some significance to the non-stop head-long society of today.

Sir Geoffrey Jellicoe
April 1986

The conservatory of Nicola Bayley's house, seen here from the doorway to the kitchen, has a cream coloured canvas blind to soften the sunlight. On top of the pianola is a ceramic bust of Queen Victoria (FAR LEFT).

In preference to its own drinking bowl, an ornamental sink makes a watering hole for the discerning family cat in Pamela Bullmore's conservatory (LEFT).

LADY ABERCONWAY

Lady Aberconway is the wife of the third Lord Aberconway.
They live at Bodnant, a half-timbered stone house in
North Wales which was altered in Victorian and Edwardian
times from the original Georgian building.

IN THE thirty-seven years I have been at Bodnant I have associated the conservatory mostly as a place for plants, and the one real exception to this has been the Easter egg hunt when the children were growing up. When it was a rainy Easter Sunday the cardboard eggs with the little presents in them were hidden amongst the leaves and in the afternoon before tea there would be a hunt. This was always the greatest fun and we have had egg hunts since for the grandchildren, but otherwise the conservatory, which adjoins the house, has not figured prominently in our social life at Bodnant. Also, one does not want people falling into the pond. We did have a housemaid once who was very, very short and once on her way through from the gun room to the office beyond, she managed to fall into the pool and before being helped out had to stand with the fish swimming around her at nose level. There are few incidents that come to mind about the conservatory because for a long time there was so little activity in it, although my father-in-law liked to go and look at the choice plants he housed in there.

However the room is being given a new lease of life. We have almost completed the refurbishment of the place for the first time since it was put up a hundred years ago. A document we found records that a glasshouse was built after 1875 and before 1886 by Messenger & Company Patentees and the Midland Horticultural Works of Loughborough, though there is no indication of which firm did what. I imagine Messenger were responsible for the design of the building. It was all part of the scheme of Mr Pochin who bought the property and who later became the father-in-law of the first Lord Aberconway. In the 1870s he followed the style of those times and changed the small Georgian house into a large one refaced in the gothicky style. At that time there were a series of Victorian working greenhouses built along the steep wall running up the hill from the house towards the garden entrance. In these were kept the precious tender plants such as orchids and camellias, but these buildings have now been pulled down.

We had often discussed doing something with the dilapidated conservatory, because it is a handsome building with a central lantern shaped like one on a pavilion and to have demolished it would have been a shame. A contract to renovate our conservatory was placed with Francis Machin and then at the 1984 Liverpool Garden Festival, where my husband was Commissioner-General, we were given an entertainment suite which was in fact a modern conservatory also built by this same designer. It was light, warm and full of flowers and made a most charming place for giving lunches and dinners. From this first-hand experience I realized the attractive potential of our own conservatory once it was made more habitable. The next step was the present given to my husband on his retirement from the Royal Horticultural Society two years ago, after being president for twenty-three years. This is a fine table with a circular top in Welsh slate and legs carved from Bodnant oak. The natural place for this piece of furniture to go seemed to be in the conservatory. The process of renovation has so far taken eighteen months.

The surface of the rectangular pond unites by its reflection two convex shapes in perfect harmony.

To return to the beginning. There are old photographs which show plants in the front hall and so it is possible Mr Pochin used the conservatory first for propagating plants to be taken into the main part of the house. Pictures also show palms in the drawing room built later in about 1902, but little more is known other than that the

Lady Aberconway seen in the reflection of an octagonal framed mirror within the conservatory (BELOW).

glass room obviously survived the neglect of maintenance during the two world wars. Much of the planting in it is original and we removed the tubs during repairs but everything is now being re-installed. We were faced with ironwork which had become badly crumbled, broken panes of glass, wood which was completely rotten and the original nineteenth-century paintwork in battle-ship grey streaked with rust. The Victorian tiles which are a deep red, thin and shiny, were happily

View of the conservatory demonstrating its comfortable link with both house and garden (LEFT).

Beside the grotto arch, a mauve Brunfelsia *and the graceful hanging* Russellia.

all in mint condition and there has been no need to repair the floor. The pond will have fish in it again eventually, and we may in the future add water-lilies growing in tubs there. There are lilies in the garden ponds and the fish will be the small golden carp, the same as those in the water outside.

The conservatory is heated by an oil heater which runs on the same system as the one heating some of the other outside garden buildings, but it is an independent circuit from the heating of the main house. About the irrigation and ventilation I know little, except that someone comes with a garden hose to do the watering and someone else decides which of the various little windows at the top of the roof to open and when. Martin Puddle who is our head gardener is in charge of the whole day-to-day routine and the planting.

The appearance of the conservatory is now altogether much cosier than before with the inside walls painted the colour of weak iced coffee – a shade which contributes an illusion of warmth and is a good foil for plants. The ironwork has been repainted white. We are looking for furniture which is compatible with the style of the conservatory and with the slate table. At present, I envisage finding a white painted iron dining table which is large enough to seat eight and then get the chairs to go with it. Ideally, I would like to have antique garden furniture, but this is not only often uncomfortable but fearfully expensive and difficult to find nowadays. One day we will find exactly what we need, and then the slate table will be used for drinks or to put books upon and the chairs will have pretty cushions in a thick, slubbed cotton – material which is just right for sitting on in a damp mac when one comes in from the garden, or for small children, if they must, to throw food onto.

One day there will be two chandeliers hung from the central struts across the conservatory and they will be easy to connect up with the electricity, but this is another item still in theory and I like to think of the evenings when we will also have meals by candlelight. The food will need careful planning in this new scheme of things, for a cheese soufflé would be flat as a flounder by the time it had been navigated from the kitchen down the passage to our plates. I can see an endless string of cold collations instead. So far we have had only a handful of people in to drinks in the newly furbished room but they have enjoyed themselves in the unusual setting and certainly the noise has not been overpowering with people on a tiled floor in a room of glass.

The two original circular metal display stands, each five-foot high, will soon be in good repair again and back in the glass room piled with potted plants. In the meantime we have a yellow mimosa which reaches almost to the roof, a most delicious scented *Jasmine polyanthum*, a lot of camellias, both old and new ones, and the sweet-smelling rhododendrons in pots – these varieties include the *R. tyermannii*, *R. maddenii* ssp. *maddenii polyandrum* group, *R. carneum* and *R. ciliicalyx*. Then there are some glorious yellow and orange clivias and a purple bougainvillea.

At the end of the room is a baby grotto which faces the door leading straight out into the garden, and beyond this grotto is another larger one or fernery. The fernery is a completely enclosed space, rather dank and dark. It has a small pool and is full of cascading ferns and some other plants including a brunfelsia which has a purple flower not entirely unlike an hibiscus. The grotto is all very well, but a little hazardous too, since the floor is made of nobbly concrete slightly on a slope leading to the pool and covered with a thick coat of green slime.

There is one other room connected to the conservatory which is referred to as the gun room, possibly the name stems from the days when it was not considered *comme il faut* to smoke at a gathering, and so guests in a shooting party would go there for a smoke after dinner. These days the place is filled with old photographs and framed floral diplomas. The general view from the conservatory windows is out onto the top lawn and over into the parkland.

When I enter the conservatory the sensation immediately conveyed by the scent is of warmth: warmth of the Mediterranean, of Greece in particular, and also of expensive bath oil. All rather luxurious. Perhaps one day I will feel like reading the Sunday newspapers in the room or curling up in there with a book on a wet day and listening to the sound of rain on the roof. And so the time has come when the conservatory will play a much more important part in our life – and the room will be enjoyed by both plants and people.

Thin sunlight on an early afternoon in winter accentuates the band of window panes in coloured glass.

STANLEY FALCONER

Stanley Falconer is a partner in the interior decoration firm of
Colefax & Fowler. His country home is a sixteenth-century
house of Cotswold stone and stone slate roof.

ON EXPLORING the south of England I found that the lovely rural countryside of the upper Cotswolds – one could be one thousand miles from London – and particularly the architecture, strongly influenced by the Huguenots, appealed to me most of all. It is now ten years since I bought this small sixteenth-century country house, having searched for three years, and although it needed many structural repairs the main original features were intact. The large garden was a complete wilderness with very little in the way of 'bones' other than a stream running along the lower part of the property, a seven-foot beech hedge and one or two mature trees – hornbeam, lovely larch, and a 'Christmas pudding' yew. However the atmosphere of the property and its rural position in very unspoilt rolling Gloucestershire countryside met my demanding requirements. These were: house to be light, spacious and private with nothing to spoil the eye, such as unfortunate housing developments or caravan sites. Of course there is always the unexpected, three years after moving in oil was discovered nearby in a particularly beautiful part. Fortunately it proved unviable, much to the relief of the village ladies who used to lie across roads to obstruct machinery!

Professionally I always advise, where possible, a getting-to-know period where one finds out how to get the best from one's property. Therefore the next two years were spent in the house as it was, planning and day-dreaming over the restoration and more daunting task of the garden plan. This

The open door leads to a courtyard which on warm days becomes a natural extension of the garden room.

period always pays dividends – so many houses and cottages have lost their character and 'guts' because of unsuitability and pretentiousness in architecture and furnishings. William Kent console tables do not belong in humble cottages! Suitability and comfort are all important.

The garden hall, as it is known, was originally a pantry containing the copper and baking oven and with a flagstone floor. It was rather depressing, with whitewashed walls and little light getting in through the pretty but north-facing small mullioned window. One of the most obvious improvements was to make a garden door from the room onto the south-facing aspect of the house. This change turned a dull rather pointless room into a sunny garden hall, and being positioned in the middle of the house it became the natural pivot of the house and garden. On one side you go into the sitting room with a snug study/bookroom beyond. On the other side is an entrance hall, dining room and kitchen. The layout of rooms is rather French in that one looks from one large chimneypiece through the four main rooms to another large chimneypiece.

The walls in the hall were glaze-painted in a warm stone-beige and around the top and bottom of the walls I copied, as a frieze, a leaf design taken from an antique painted screen, bought in Bath. There are a number of examples of this type of hand-painted work on ceilings and walls in the area. This is mainly thanks to the rich woolmerchants of the seventeenth and eighteenth centuries who demanded fine homes and interiors to compete with the gentry.

Previously I had leased a mill-house in Sussex where over several years I collected some interesting wood and painted English and French country

furniture. All of these pieces fitted perfectly into Tughill. I had a number of fine German botanical drawings in painted frames and this was the perfect place to hang them. Likewise the three fruitwood French country armchairs and writing desk were just right for the garden room. Later on my old friend and partner John Fowler left me the pretty and very unusual plant table, which he bought from Syrie Maugham before the last war. This is always covered and surrounded by various and changing pot plants – scented-leaved geraniums, streptocarpus, ivy, cyclamen and sparmannia in painted *cache-pot*, rush and wicker baskets. Original to the room was an L-shaped shelf over the low mullioned window, which when cleared of jam jars and stripped of paint revealed a warm fruitwood. This now holds a collection of carved wood treen fruits, painted pigeons and duck decoys, and a Noah's Ark of little wooden animals.

In the summer sitting in the garden hall became a way of life. While sitting here over breakfast, tea or drinks we started seriously to plan the garden. Three feet away from the garden door there ran a dry-stone wall the length of the house, which held back a steep overgrown bank looking up towards the roof of a tiny early nineteenth-century Methodist chapel. Not without some difficulty, and some hysterics over a yellow earth remover as tall as the house, we pushed the bank back fifteen feet in order to create a very sunny and private forty-five foot long flagstoned terrace with steps up to the garden. This improvement complemented the garden hall and the terrace became an outdoor room on which we have on occasions had to take refuge from the heat in the hall.

After many visits to interesting and charming gardens and houses in the vicinity – Stanway, Hidcote, Kiftsgate, Kelmscott – we drew up plans

Seen from the adjoining dining room a small writing desk; on the wall three framed flower prints, a shelf with a collection of wooden animals and life-size wooden pigeon, a tapestry bell-pull to left.

and ideas which were pinned up, discussed, not to say argued over, altered and improved upon over many months. To complete the view from the garden hall we laid a generous grass path between two herbaceous borders edged with lavender interspersed with box mopheads, looking up to a stone shepherd boy surrounded by a semi-circle of yew hedge. This is backed by lime trees, inquisitive sheep grazing over the wall and the chapel beyond.

Through the hall window one looks across a formal box garden, with a mixture of golden and green box in four quarters centred on a sundial, and beyond towards a charming tack house. This

A carved wood poodle dog sits on the garden room matting with a view through to the dining room and sitting room beyond.

whole area is surrounded by a six-foot drystone wall forming a lovely sheltered courtyard, the walls being smothered with roses, honeysuckle, vine, japonica, climbing hydrangea and akebia.

Even in winter, and especially during a snowy Christmas when the room is lit by candles on the tree and pussy-cats are fascinated by wrappings and parcels, it's a joy!

HUGH JOHNSON

*Writer and editor Hugh Johnson is the author of several books on wine,
trees and gardening. He writes about gardening
as 'Tradescant' in* The Garden, *the magazine of the
Royal Horticultural Society and in the* New York Times.
*His wife Judy is a graphic designer and printer and they live with
their three children at Saling Hall, a seventeenth-century
manor house in north Essex.*

THE CONSERVATORY at Saling was planned and replanned, drawn and torn up and drawn again, for five years before it was built. It was not that we didn't know what sort of conservatory we wanted, or where. The hesitation was out of diffidence in adding anything to a seventeenth-century building which we thought was, in its simple way, perfect. The house has a tall plain chequer-brick side facing south-west over its brick-walled garden: the ideal place to build a sun-trap, its back to the cold spring winds that are a speciality of eastern England. But the sheer rightness of that wall, with its rhythm of fifteen mullioned windows, inhibited us.

The break-through came when we realized that it would forgive an addition as bold and plain as itself, echoing its length and proportions, lying alongside like a spanking new tender to a grand old liner, or a glossy young foal to a draught horse.

After that the constraints were all positively helpful. The height was decided by the ledges of the first-floor windows: there had to be space below them for a nine-inch lead covered beam to weld the conservatory to the house. Given the maximum height, the necessary minimum pitch to the roof, and proper height under the gutter for a door on the garden side, the maximum possible

A glimpse of the conservatory from the gateway leading to the kitchen garden. Formal clipped box beds border the brick path.

width was ten feet. To take full advantage of the house wall, with the interruptions of two doors and two windows, we needed five bays out of the eight, or forty feet. In elevation, forty feet by fourteen exactly echoed the bulk of the house with its steep tiled roof.

A sense of modesty, rather than pastiche, decided that the new building should look as much as possible as though our Victorian predecessors had perpetrated it. They invented the conservatory, so we could hardly attribute it to remoter forebears.

The Victorians also used the sort of firm, well-defined details that make a thin glass structure feel like architecture. The differences may look slight on the plans, but in real light and shade they are enormous. We based our plans on an off-the-shelf modular conservatory made by Amdega of Darlington. But whereas the standard model has thin flat glazing bars we specified deep moulded ones like any Victorian window. And the thin cornice and plastic guttering proposed were no good for our purposes. We added in a six-inch beam for depth in the cornice, bought cast-iron ogee guttering, and gave our local builder a nightmare by commissioning one hundred and forty hand-carved little wooden brackets as dentils to give life and importance to the eaves – the most important part of any building, as the Greeks, Romans, Goths and Italians knew, but modern architects still often forget.

What I forgot was that a deep and handsome cornice above the windows deserved a similar sill

A quiet place for reading with jasmine, pelargoniums and Acacia parvissima *growing against the brick wall.*

to cast a strong shadow on the pink bricks of the lower walls. The mingy modern sill is the one clear give-away: the hand-made bricks from the Bulmer Tye brickworks near Sudbury are ageless.

The single greatest decision in planning the inside was whether to have a hard floor throughout and use pots for all plants, or to leave beds through into the earth beneath, or to make artificial beds either built up from, or sunk into, the floor. The advantage of beds is that plants in them can grow to luxuriant sizes, and also that established plants can go unwatered for days at a time. The counter-vailing advantage of pots is that you can keep swopping them round; enjoy winter-flowering plants, for example, and then move them outdoors (where they would much rather be) for the sum-mer. With the help of a separate 'working' green-house you can have a year-round supply of fresh plants in fine fettle. The great disadvantage of pots, of course, is that they need watering, some-times even twice a day. I would not counsel pots unless you are always at home, or have a regular gardener.

In the end we chose pots and a hard floor, tiled with foot-square clay tiles very like the old Essex 'pammets' but made in Spain. For drainage we sank a foot-wide channel all round, with a slight fall to one end. We searched for decorative cast-iron gratings – and found a solitary one rusting in a builder's yard. To our amazement a small foundry in the next-door village of Rayne undertook to copy it, and did so perfectly. The gratings cover the drainage channel, and most of the pots find places on or near it. Those that stand in the middle of the floor stand on big clay saucers.

The conservatory embraces the old garden door from the hall of the house, one bay from its southern end. The door lies on the main axis of the garden, an importance we stressed in designing the conservatory by putting double doors in its side on this axis. It also embraces the two windows of the little sitting room next to the kitchen, which has certainly gained an extra charm by looking out into the conservatory, even if it has lost some of its natural light. What used to be a window in the kitchen we converted into a fully-glazed door into the conservatory, leading to the end where a round glass-topped table and five chairs (all white, all Lloyd-loom) make a natural café for breakfast among the plants. A leaded-light panel above this kitchen door was painted for us by the artist Jane Gray with four of our favourite flowers for four seasons: the crown imperial, Corsican hellebore, blue agapanthus and white Japanese anemone.

Under its sheltering south-west wall the con-servatory would overheat unbearably without good shading and ventilation. The top light opens along the whole length by winding one handle by

A view of the glass panel painted by Jane Gray of four favourite plants framed by vines.

the kitchen door. All the side panels are hinged at the top and open on brass stays. Most important of all, the shading is outside the glass: the cedar lath roller blinds interrupt the sunlight before it ever reaches the glass. I love the striped-light effect they give.

What do we grow in our pots? Nothing very fanciful, I'm afraid, but the standard tender plants that create a vaguely Mediterranean atmos-

phere: in summer blue plumbago and dark red passion flowers, geraniums galore, fuchsias (which would prefer somewhere cooler and damper), lilies, the buff rose Maréchal Niel, and many plants just for their foliage: lyonothamnus, *Grevillea robusta*, *Mahonia lomariifolia*, ferns and even wispy bamboos.

In autumn we bring in from outside pots of oranges and lemons (Meyer's is the only one that fruits regularly), an olive, and a great gleaming dome of *Camellia sasanqua*, pink-flowering all winter. Australian plants, acacias and prostanthera, are especially valuable in winter, and eucalyptus all year round. Perhaps the best regular winter feature is the flowering together of a bright purple sage, *Salvia ambigens* var. *caerulea* (a present from Knightshayes Court in Devon), that clambers gamely up into the roof, with yellow *Mahonia lomariifolia* and creamy *Acacia podalyriifolia*. With luck *Nandina domestica* will be carrying some scarlet berries.

This amount of winter flower is achieved by simply keeping the frost out. Our only heating is by two three-kilowatt fan heaters on thermostats set at 40° F. They circulate the air briskly, which I am sure the plants enjoy. Their big disadvantage is the noise they make – but when it is warm enough to tempt one to dawdle they turn themselves off.

We have a tap at each end of the conservatory, supplied with rain-water pumped up to a tank in the roof, and fitted with a hose just long enough to reach all the pots. In winter a watering can is a better and more precise way of watering, but in summer I fill the pots to the brim and a hose saves many minutes a day.

I must mention the two residents: a little white marble Bacchus with his pet leopard, and a huge plaster bust of Zeus. To me their classical presence adds something that plants alone cannot provide. They add emphasis to the rhythm of white bars that form the building; they stress the human element, the essential artificiality of a plant house that depends on keeping natural forces firmly under control.

Striped with shadows cast by the cedar blinds above, Hugh and Julia Johnson breakfast by a stone statue of Bacchus.

THE EARL OF HARROWBY

*The sixth Earl of Harrowby lives at Sandon Hall, the family
seat in Staffordshire. Lord Harrowby, who is a widower,
is in his ninety-fourth year.*

I DON'T REMEMBER coming here until I was
eight years old; that was in 1900, after my
father succeeded. Before that, the house had
belonged to my great-uncle, the third Earl. He
died on 26 March 1900 and, as he had no children,
was succeeded by my grandfather. But my grandfather was himself a very sick man and was on a
cruise at the time, trying to regain his health. He
died, eight and a half months later, in December
1900, and never came here as Earl of Harrowby.

My father became the fifth Earl when he was
thirty-six years old and my mother, who was the
youngest daughter of W.H.Smith, was thirty-
three. They had a lot of work done to the house,
grounds and estate generally, but we came here
straight away. Our time was divided between
Sandon and our London and Gloucestershire
homes. The house was usually full of visitors as my
mother loved entertaining. Although my elder
sister and I were the only surviving children, we
had masses of uncles, aunts and cousins on both
sides; my father had three brothers and four sisters
and my mother one brother and four sisters.
Added to that there were strong political connec-
tions in every generation until my children's;
several members of the family held ministerial
posts.

The present Sandon Hall is the third, the second
on this site. It overlooks the Trent valley with
parkland to the north and formal gardens to the
south. The previous, Georgian, house was burnt
down in 1848 and the present house was completed

in 1853. The conservatory and adjoining bell tower
were built thirteen years later, in 1866, by my
great-grandfather, the second Earl. To help pay
for 'The Great Conservatory', three fine Sèvres
vases were sold for £1,500 – we have photographs
of the vases, but have been unable to trace them.
The total cost appears to have been £7,396.6.10,
exclusive of the architect's fees; this figure, however, includes the bell tower and other alterations
to the house.

Architects: MESSRS STEVENS & ROBINSON OF DERBY

	£	s	d
Stone: quarried in the Park	24	2	6
Wrought iron from Charles Smith of Birmingham	1,065	16	4
Hanging bell	207	10	0
Builders: Warburton Brothers of Manchester............................	5,254	15	1
Encaustic tiles: Minton Hollins & Co, Patent Tile Works, Stoke on Trent	126	16	0
Hales: Glass...........................	303	9	5
Weekes:Heating.......................	354	15	0
Shears: Bell	59	2	6

My great-grandparents, particularly my great-
grandmother, who was a daughter of the Marquis
of Bute, spent a lot of time on the continent,
especially Italy. Although she died in 1859, it may
be her influence which inspired the 'Italianate'
elements of the design – however, I do believe that
such 'rooms' were the fashion of the day.

The conservatory was designed by Messrs
Stevens & Robinson of Derby. It is a rectangular
building on an east-west axis, joined to the house
by a quarter circle passageway which comes out of
the foot of the bell tower at the north-east corner

*View from the main entrance into the conservatory where
some of the shrubs date from the original 19th century
planting.*

Detail shows the beautiful ironwork and paint which, with their surroundings, evoke the romance of the Victorian era.

of the house. The passageway enables it to be sited to the north of the house, balancing the single-storey west wing and forming the third side of the front court. The stone is the same as that of the house and was quarried in the park. A balustraded double staircase leads from the front court up to the main door. Shrubberies hide the windowless north and east walls. Behind the shrubs there is a small staircase which leads down to the crypt, where a boiler supplies the under-floor heating. On the south side the floor to ceiling windows are framed by climbing roses and a vine – though it only produces very small grapes which seldom sweeten enough to eat. Planted borders separate the window from a raised terrace retained by a wall.

If you enter the conservatory from the house you pass through a heavy wooden door into the curved passageway. On your left is the bell-rope for the bell tower. The bell was rung, except in wartime, until the 1960s as a five-minute warning for lunch and thirty minutes for dinner, to allow time for changing into evening dress. The empty niches to right and left contained statues in the classical style, which are now in the front hall. The ceiling and right-hand wall of the passage are glazed. The wall on the left looks beautiful when the fuchsias are out. Along the wall and across the ceiling is a lovely old wisteria – there is another, even bigger, in the orangery at the end of the rose garden. Along the walls on either side you see the elaborate wrought-iron grilles beneath which the central-heating pipes run. At the end of the passage are two small glazed doors which lead down a couple of steps to the conservatory and library terraces.

If you turn to the left you enter the conservatory proper. On the wall you will see a map of the garden which was drawn by my wife who was very fond of the gardens. Further on to the left is the main door to the front court with a mosaic 'SALVE' on the floor, and straight ahead is a large window through which, looking north-west you see the park, the ice-house plantation and the Trent valley, where river, canal, railway and road run within a hundred yards of each other.

Now if you turn to your right you are looking down the full length of the conservatory. The wrought-iron pillars combined with columns delineate a nave and two aisles. In the centre of the far wall is a looking-glass in which the length of the conservatory is reflected. Beneath the glass is a goldfish basin, which from the other end looks like an altar. In the basin there is a fountain, which used to play continually, reaching almost to the roof. The last goldfish died some years ago. It was very fat and old; we were convinced that it had eaten all its fellows.

The two aisles are given over to flower beds. Otherwise, the floor is mosaic, with a monochrome background broken up by circles and other geometrical shapes. Placed down the nave are several marble inlaid tables. The best, an Adam one, had to be sold a few years ago. Some of us used to sit in large square wicker chairs, with attached footrests

underneath which pulled out, and backs which could have their positions altered so that, if you wished, you could lie full length. We still have some of these chairs, though I doubt if they would be safe to sit in any more.

Halfway down the conservatory on the left is an alcove. There used to be a sofa all the way round its wall and a table would be placed in the middle for my mother to pour out tea. On the walls of the alcove were two Assyrian plaques which my great-uncle, the third Earl, when he was Lord Sandon brought back in 1853 from an archaeological dig with Lord Carnarvon. They were from the North West Palace of King Ashurnaserpal II in Nimrud (883–859 BC). Unfortunately we had to sell these treasures a few years ago.

The vaulting of the sloping glazed roof is wrought iron. The wall on the alcove side is stone,

Snaking its way around the entrance from the conservatory, an ancient wisteria grows on into the curved passage.

painted a Mediterranean blue. It is possibly the paint from my childhood which remains today, though it is peeling away. I also remember large blue jars, some with plants placed on them.

From the alcove you look out over the lawn tennis court, or would do if the flowers didn't hide the view. The court is down a steep bank from the library terrace. At one time it was, I believe, considered one of the best courts in the county. It was the pride and joy of our head gardener who maintained that no-one could find a single weed on it. This gardener was brought in as a youngish man by my father when he succeeded, as were several senior estate employees, and he stayed with him till he retired forty-five years later, having seen out the ravages of two world wars.

My mother loved flowers and gardens and spent many hours planning improvements, particularly to the shrubberies. In those days we had masses of gardeners, over twenty at the beginning of the century, so all the actual gardening she ever did was to cut off dead heads.

When I was a boy the conservatory was not much used in the summer but it was somewhat of a winter ritual to have Sunday tea here. My mother and the other ladies dressed for it as if they were in the tropics, in long spotted muslins with flowing ribbons. The conservatory was kept so hot because it was full of exotic plants, strong scented crotons, beautifully coloured tropical flowers (no camellias then, it was too hot), bananas and oranges (though these only fruited occasionally) and palms. The excessive heat was given up during the first war, though the real cut down took place in the thirties with the financial crisis. After that the conservatory was used more in summer on windy days, or on sunny days in spring and autumn. The heating now is only just sufficient to keep off the frost, but we still have some lovely flowers, particularly two camellias which reach up to the roof on either side of the alcove. One is white, the other pink and they flower for about three months in the winter. We also have an hydrangea which produces enormous flowers, not to mention the pelargoniums and fuchsias.

Outside near the conservatory a timeless, noble beast ponders.

We have no record of the famous people who visited the conservatory. Princess Beatrice stayed in 1903, the Prince of Wales visited in 1924, Prince Henry (later Duke of Gloucester) in 1927 and Princess Mary (the Princess Royal) in 1930 and 1932, but all these visits took place in the summer. The first great party I remember was the visit of the colonial prime ministers in 1902. Of the British politicians who visited during my lifetime the most eminent was Joseph Chamberlain in 1906. Our last great party was a visit of International Ex-Allied and Ex-Enemy Ex-Servicemen in 1936. This was an attempt at reconciliation which could not prevent the Second World War. A photograph was taken of them all on the steps of the conservatory and trees were planted in the garden on behalf of each participating country and joined together with white ribbons of peace and other ribbons in the national colours. Few of these trees survived.

After my wife and I moved here in 1958 we were only able to use the conservatory very occasionally because of staff shortages, but sometimes my wife had tea here, for instance at Christmas for the estate workers' children. It was also used each June when the annual Cadet Garden Party was held at Sandon and many times it was the scene of a coffee morning held in aid of charity. Nowadays it is only used for serving teas when charitable functions are held in the grounds or sometimes family occasions like house parties for cricket matches.

The difficulty is to keep it rain-proof. Various storms have taken their toll, like the one in January 1975 when about two hundred trees were lost in the garden and another two hundred in the park, and much of the conservatory glass was damaged. Again, only a short time ago, just after the glass roof had been repaired, a strong gust of wind blew in one north-facing window, next to the main door, and the resulting draught lifted a whole lot of the roof glass, so repairs had to begin all over again. Yet, in spite of a leaking roof, limited heating and almost non-existent labour, it is still, given favourable weather conditions, a very pleasant place in which to sit.

The curved passage way leading from the house to conservatory, viewed from the end of the grass tennis court.

THE HON. CHRISTOPHER McLAREN

The Hon. Christopher McLaren is the youngest son of the late Lord and Lady Aberconway. With his wife Janey and two children he lives in London and at Maenan, their country house in the Conway valley, North Wales. The house has a seventeenth- and eighteenth-century stone façade and the back is fifteenth century with Elizabethan plasterwork.

IN THE AUTUMN of 1962 my late mother, Lady Aberconway, for whom my father had bought Maenan as a dower house, conceived the idea of an exterior 'sun room' whence she could admire the garden and the view without risking the effects of the Welsh weather. Clough Williams-Ellis, the architect and creator of Portmeirion, was a longtime family friend, so who better was there to design her sun room. Indeed he had just completed for her a summerhouse, some twenty miles away on his own estate, known as 'The Drum House'. This had come about when Clough had heard that my mother was seeking a site for a summerhouse, where she could arrange picnic luncheons for her guests, and had offered to find a suitable position and build upon it to her command.

He referred on occasions to the sun room as 'Christabel's Casket' and 'your golden bower', but it became known as the 'Crystal Room'. The overall design relates to the chinoiserie furniture and tapestry in the then dining room of the house, which the Crystal Room adjoins. My mother was insistent that the roof and walls of the room should be of perspex and not of glass lest a slate should fall from the roof of the house and, shattering the glass, injure the occupants. The perspex roof panels have in fact developed a greenish patina under the influence of the Welsh weather, which some regard as pleasing. There was an idea, not

The north-west facing front of the house seen from the lower garden across the sweeping lawn.

followed up, that there should be curtains similar to those around a four-poster bed. There are, however, powerful electric heating rails which can warm it up extremely quickly, even in coldest winter. On one occasion, these were accidentally left on for over a month, with a most unfortunate effect upon the electricity bill.

The Crystal Room was designed for, and used as, an outdoor room in which to sit, read, talk, work or from which just to admire the sky and the view. It was never a conservatory as such as the only plants that I can remember there were a sweet geranium and then, for a short time, a datura and now, every summer, morning glory. It was furnished with two easy chairs and five of a set of Georgian cane-backed wooden chairs. There are also two glass-topped tables, one small and octagonal containing a marvellous pink Victorian shell arrangement. A nineteenth-century watercolour of a Chinese stood there for many years, and it is remarkable that this never faded.

The room was made and erected in May 1963 by Henry Hope & Sons of Smethwick, and very well they did too. I have no record of the cost and the fact that the two finials were purchased locally in Portmadoc for five shillings each is hardly a guide. There is, however, a letter from my mother to the firm saying how much admiration the room had attracted, but that when she said how much it had cost, her hearers had gone strangely silent.

When Janey and I took over the house following my mother's death in 1974, we had to make some rearrangement of the internal rooms in order to

The design of the 'Crystal Room', erected in 1963, echoes the chinoiserie furniture and a tapestry in the old dining room of the house.

accommodate our children. The Crystal Room became even more essential as we had decided to use the Elizabethan plasterwork hall at the back of the house as our dining room. This, as one would expect from its date, does not have expansive windows and as it does not give on to a fine view it can be rather gloomy at lunchtime on a sunny day. Thus the Crystal Room became an auxiliary dining room: for lunch on all days except the very

wettest, or unless there were more than six or eight people present, and for dinner on fine summer evenings, when it is rarely warm enough to sit out. Although it is simple to carry out food from the kitchen, moisture sometimes breeds algae on the slightly uneven surface which becomes formidably slippery, particularly to those essaying the short journey from the house bearing a tray laden with plates or glasses.

It is the greatest pleasure, when one has escaped from London, to be able to sit and eat effectively *en plein air* and to enjoy the changing delights of the garden, of the hills and of the sky. The pleasure of sitting and sampling by direct contact a garden and countryside as clouds replace sunshine and calm gives way to wind, and vice versa, usually eludes one in Britain. This pleasure seldom eludes us at Maenan, and thereby the Crystal Room enormously increases our enjoyment. It creates an ideal compromise between sheltering behind thick and ancient stone walls from a blustery Celtic winter and being able to eat *al fresco* under a scorching summer sun.

We usually have Christmas lunch in the Crystal Room – providing we are not too many. By eating relatively austerely at lunchtime we are able to capitalize on the few hours of winter daylight and to save our energies for Christmas dinner, at which time over-indulgence does not ruin the rest of the day and after which we have time to sleep off its effects. Often (or is it just on the occasions that one remembers?) the sun shines with a warm almost horizontal yellow light casting long shadows across the lawn, and the effect is the more precious for its brief existence.

The Crystal Room stands at the back left corner of the York stone terrace, which runs the full width in front of the house and divides the façade from the rectangular lawn. The lawn itself faces north-west and is flanked by yew hedges which terminate in a pair of magnificent lead sphinxes on four-foot stone plinths. Between and below these runs a parapet wall, invisible from the house, which supports the end of the lawn. The view across the lawn gives first onto ornamental trees, backed by oaks and beeches and then beyond the Conway valley on to the Carnedd mountains. The clouds form and re-form across the wide sweep of sky under which the light constantly changes.

Morning glory grows along the metalwork framing a view of the foothills of the Carnedds.

Conservatory on a terrace of York stone with a border of lavender and a Magnolia grandiflora *growing against the façade of the house.*

The terrace adds greatly to the amenity of the house and provides truly outdoor accommodation when the weather allows. It is backed by a lavender hedge against the front of the house, of which part of the façade was built in the eighteenth century and the other part in the early nineteenth century as an exact match. *Magnolia grandiflora, Ceanothus thyrsiflorus* 'Cascade' and various clematis grow up the façade so that on a hot August day the air is redolent with magnolia

and lavender scent and resonates to the drone of bumble bees.

I have referred to the 'Drum House' which, like the Crystal Room, was only a part of the collaboration between Clough Williams-Ellis and my parents and later with my mother. It was so called, as it was a restored winding-house on a disused slate quarry railway and had contained a vast drum around which the cable which hauled the trucks was wound. Clough, having obtained planning consent on the basis of 'saving' an ancient monument, converted it into an imposing single room for picnics or camp-bed holidays. His own eightieth birthday was celebrated there on 1 June 1963, just after the completion of the Crystal Room, in glorious weather and in dazzling company.

My father had bought Maenan Hall, some six miles south of my parents' house at Bodnant, in 1946. My father's agent had previously written that he had agreed a price of £4,392 for the house and two hundred acres of farm land and that 'I am satisfied that he [the Vendor] will not come down by one penny'! The house, now a Grade I listed building, had been used for the previous twenty-five years as a farmhouse and was in a terrible state. Much of the front, built in the eighteenth and early nineteenth centuries, was occupied by the farmer, but my father was able to restore the back part, a fifteenth-century timber frame building with seventeenth-century roof and walls and with magnificent Elizabethan plasterwork. Part of the plasterwork had fallen from the ceiling of the double storey hall to the floor, and it was Clough who provided a skilled plasterer from Portmeirion.

After my father died in 1953, my mother was able to obtain possession of the whole house and to modernize it. In 1956 she moved in and despite financial uncertainties was never deterred from a continual programme of development and building, explaining to me that what had always appeared to be her greatest extravagances had turned out to be her greatest economies.

She began by building a magnificent garage, complete with gardeners' sheds where there had been pigsties and then proceeded to renovate the old tower a quarter of a mile up the hill from Maenan. At that time, it consisted merely of a massive circular stone wall, two storeys in height, held together by a huge ivy. The tower was struck one night by lightning, and became dangerous, so that the only options were destruction or rehabilitation. My mother naturally chose the latter and installed a delightful furnished room at first-floor level and a magnificent eight-foot Venetian statue of Bacchus below. Thus the tower itself became a garden room, except in the sense that it is beyond, though overlooking, the garden and it was returned to something close to its original

function as an eighteenth-century folly (there is, however, an unsubstantiated theory that it had started life as a watch tower in the fourteenth century or earlier).

Whilst the Crystal Room was being manufactured, my mother and Clough were developing further plans, this time to erect an obelisk up to sixty-feet high on a hill above the drive at Maenan. She had been inspired to do this as a wish to imitate, even if not to rival, the column in Anglesey commemorating the first Marquess, but the estimated costs were too high. I remember Clough trying to encourage her, saying that it could be made with a pipe up the middle and that when she died her ashes (she was always determined to be cremated and not to lie mouldering in the ground, and she was much concerned about what would happen to her ashes after her death), could be blown out of the top by an electric pump and dissipated by the winds over the surrounding Welsh countryside. Even this did not persuade her.

Her building proclivities continued until she tried to have a circular piece of marshy land above the house excavated to form a pond. The consistency of the mud and the lack of firm base beneath almost proved too much for the earth-moving equipment of the day, and although she was not defeated, she did say that she would not build anything further. And she stuck to her word.

However, of all these embellishments in and around Maenan, it is the Crystal Room that has proved much the most important to our lives. It is the Crystal Room which for us turns foul weather into fair and night into day. It is views from the Crystal Room of the garden and mountains that come to mind when we are in London and we wish that Maenan was not two hundred miles away. It is the Crystal Room which enables us to extract full value from the Maenan part of our life. I recommend such a folly to all who bemoan the British weather.

The owner and his children in the glass house which is entered through double sliding doors. The George III wood and cane-back garden chairs are from Bodnant and painted to simulate bamboo; the floor matting comes from Habitat, and the printed material is by Warners.

JAMES RUSSELL

James Russell is a landscape designer and plantsman. He lives at The Dairies on the Castle Howard Estate in Yorkshire.

THE GARDEN ROOM is the most important room in my life since I use it all the time and all the year round. Perhaps because I am a landscape gardener it is the expression of a need for space and also a different environment in which it is easier to envisage landscapes which do not yet exist.

Now that my main work is on the arboretum and landscape at Castle Howard, it has also to house the many files in which careful record is kept of the ever-increasing number of species which we grow here, and the large number of Floras and other books of reference in which they need to be checked.

In the winter months my secretary and I have the room to ourselves and this is when new additions are entered and correspondence and plans for the ensuing year take place. We are building up very large collections of trees and shrubs, rhododendrons and roses, both the species and the so-called 'old' roses, and accurate records are as important as the plants.

Life in the garden room in winter is serious; in the summer it becomes much more frivolous. By mid-March the tea roses are out in the greenhouse and the canal is full of green and white arum lilies. By April garden visitors begin to appear and, as the dining room in the house is very small, we often eat in the garden room where the table will seat sixteen. On gala occasions (very rare) we bring any remaining candelabra and two big gilt torchères from the drawing room and eat by candlelight.

The construction of the room is as simple as possible and from necessity was very inexpensive.

An atmosphere created by a mixture of exotic plants and a place for quiet repose contrasts with the English garden surroundings outside.

The floor is cement and the walls are 'stone-faced' breezeblock. The large Victorian windows cost four pounds each from a bombed site in the suburbs, and the roof is the same tomato-house structure as the greenhouse, of which it is part. Inside, the walls are unpainted plaster with a pretty Gothick cornice from Mr Salter of Leeds, and a trellis to hide the glass roof. The floor is simulated marble tiles. It is heated by warm air from the greenhouse. In 1968 this did not cost very much.

As I feel that garden rooms should reflect the garden and be a link to it rather than to the house, furniture is sparse but large. There is a table painted in *trompe l'oeil* in 1950 by Goor. This is twelve feet long and five feet wide, made from a Scots pine felled at the Sunningdale Nurseries during the war, and covered in match-boarding. It is supported on plaster legs also designed by Goor.

As the room itself is forty feet by fifteen feet this does not look too large in scale and is the right size for the large plans which need to be unfolded on it, and the large numbers of Floras and files which often need to be spread out.

Down the greenhouse side there is a pair of stone tables, perhaps the original 'dairy tables' from the house. When we came here they were pushed together in one of the small annex rooms. They support a pair of graceful marble vases in the style of Canova. In the centre is a fine seventeenth-century copy of the head of Menelaus from the Vatican. The two sphinx seats were made by Goor in plaster and cast in white cement. The table, marbles and the seats are all from an earlier room at the Sunningdale Nurseries.

The other side of the room has plaster casts of the British Museum busts of Antoninus Pius, who was proclaimed in York, and Septimius Severus who died there in AD 211. There are also two gilt baroque chairs, probably Spanish. These are very decorative and are really here because they are too uncomfortable to sit on for long. There are simple bookcases at the ends of the room, also from another house which we lived in in the past, which are rapidly filling up with the Floras and other reference books.

This room is very light and airy but has its disadvantages. The roof is very apt to leak and my sister and I always dread a thunder-storm during a large luncheon party. Then it becomes extremely hot in midsummer and as cold in midwinter. However these are hazards which greenhouse dwellers must expect.

The garden room looks directly into the greenhouse, past a very charming baroque statue of Pallas Athene, down a forty foot canal to a kneeling slave table and some eighteenth-century seats and chairs; beyond is a bamboo jungle. This house is a hundred and ten feet long and forty feet wide. Originally it was planted as a tropical jungle and was very exotic with clumps of the tortoiseshell-leaved banana, and the pink-fruited banana. Ropes of brilliant passion flowers hung from the roof and there were a lot of palm trees and tree-ferns. Large artificial trees held colonies of bromeliads, hoyas and all sorts of gesneriads. Since the oil crisis the climate has cooled down to just above freezing in winter. The tree-ferns remain and so do a surprising number of bromeliads which will stand low temperatures if kept very dry in the winter.

The garden room is not connected to the house but is very close. It is entered by a door in a blank wall and all the windows except one look into the greenhouse. The Yorkshire landscape is on a huge scale and when an icy wind blows across the snowfields it is nice to be able to walk into an area which has a southern feel about it and where plenty of lush greenery can be seen.

I left school in 1938 at the age of 18 and was fortunate to be able to spend a year on the Continent. The impact of leaving this grey northern climate and waking up in Provence with its brilliant sky, dazzling buildings and the dark needle spires of the cypress, has never been forgotten. Italy was to make a deeper impression. I spent some three months in Rome staying with a cousin whose husband was at the British Embassy. This was just after the excavation of the 'House of

Livia' at Prima Porta, and I became fascinated by the Roman fashion of bringing the garden into the house with charming frescoes of flowers, plants and birds.

Pompeii and Herculaneum deepened the impression. On the way back we stayed with Captain and Mrs Warre at Roquebrune and I visited Major Johnston's garden, Serre de la Madonne, at Menton-Garavan, for the first time. These two gardens were full of wonderful exotic plants collected from Yunnan, Mexico, South Africa and Australia, growing with luxuriance in a formal setting amongst splendid urns, pots and statues.

This influence has remained and shows itself in a passion for arbutus and ilex, terracotta pots and fine marbles, and undoubtedly influenced the design of both my garden rooms. The first of these, at Sunningdale Nurseries, was a converted cowshed and there the walls were frescoed by Goor in a scheme which included the table, the sphinx seats and some of the marbles, so that elements of the first garden room continue in the second.

As this room looks into, and is connected to, the greenhouse, I do not grow any plants in it but bring in large pots from time to time. There is a wide variety of these: green-glazed Cantonese pots in several shapes and sizes, a pair of splendid Jarres d'Anduzes with their greeny-brown glaze flaking off the terracotta base, a set of the Compton Pottery terracottas to a Lutyens design from Roman originals, a number of French and Italian terracottas and a pair of French orchid pots.

There are also glazed pots by Alan Caiger Smith of the Aldermaston Pottery. Some of these are his version of the French orchid pots and were designed for an orangery at the Ideal Home Exhibition of 1963. There is an immense range of plants to put in these, perhaps citrus fruits, daturas, jasmine and ginger lilies are the favourites. There are many scented plants in the greenhouse itself, starting with the rich spicy smell of *Sarcococca confusa*, some ten feet high against the wall, and becoming more varied as the temperature rises. If there is time, and room, I grow humeas, lilies and lots of the scented tobacco plants to go into the

Work in progress on the conservatory table with a view through to the canal framed by a fine window.

A detail of plants and statue at the edge of the canal.

various pots. The greenhouse opens into the propagating house, full at the moment of seeds collected in Bhutan, China, Ecuador, Kashmir, Mexico and Nepal, waiting, once they grow, to be recorded in the garden room.

A general view of the interior of the conservatory-cum-workroom of a plantsman owner.

ANDREW LOGAN

*Andrew Logan is a jewellery designer and sculptor and a
graduate of the Oxford School of Architecture. There have been
several exhibitions of his work. His studio is a renovated glasshouse
on the top floor of a warehouse in the City of London.*

THE GLASSHOUSE IN THE SKY was first discovered in a rarely remembered dream I had in 1979 – a dream that revealed a studio of glass, with glass doors and furniture and shelves. This is now a reality save for the furniture. I took the premises on in 1980 with Michael Davis, a friend of mine who is an interior designer. The whole place had been used as a darkroom with the glass walls painted black and silver, but with the help of friends and relations we brought the glasshouse to a gleaming white crystal.

The glasshouse is fifteen hundred square feet and sits on a roof area of five thousand square feet. I think it was constructed in the 1920s, as indicated by a cap removed from the sprinkler system, and most likely it was used as a film studio before Hollywood days or as an early camera studio. It does not have opening vents or other characteristics of greenhouse construction.

Michael and myself decided that I would create the inner space and he the terraces. I am a prolific sculptor. In five years I have filled the studio with sculpture that hangs from the ceiling and packs the floor and I now have a limited space in which to work and have had to be inventive as to storage and display. The studio is south-facing and all the walls are glass, save for the north which holds a long gallery of my friends' work, including paintings by Duggie Fields, David Hockney and Adrian George. There is a small kitchenette area on the western side of the studio with an entertainment area under the gallery that at present holds more storage. Access to the garden is from all sides through various sized windows-cum-doors. Thus the garden consists of three terraces: the good-morning terrace on the east with a view of Liverpool Street Station, the lunchtime terrace to the south with a view of the City of London, dominated by the National Westminster Bank tower, and a western sunset terrace looking to the Barbican tower development. Above all this is the vast expanse of sky that dominates all views from inside the studio.

My sculptures have always incorporated sound and have taken plant forms. The fifteen foot six arum lily record player completed in 1972 was the first, then a nine-foot high mirrored palm tree with a large intertwining glory flower was built in 1975 – this held a cassette player. The third was the tree of life that sits in the studio sprouting both music and portraits of friends and relations. I built this for my 'Goddesses' exhibition at the Commonwealth Institute in 1983–4. This piece also incorporated two live love-birds that sang in the tree and these now live alongside five budgies housed in an indoor/outdoor aviary. Their songs are heard throughout the day, especially when Maria Callas is played and they join in, and their birdcage is tucked behind a life-sized Pegasus to remind them that horses can fly.

The room literally 'grew' as sculptures and plants were placed. Plants grow profusely inside the glasshouse: a phoenix palm collected from the South of France, a rubber plant ten foot high loves the climate and this year blazing pink bougainvillea showered over one section of the studio. The

*The atmosphere of an inviting woodland glade is created
on a rooftop towering over the city.*

passion flower would have reached the ceiling except for the escape of the love-birds who almost devoured the plant before being recaptured. It seems to be a race against time to see what will fill the studio first – plants or sculpture.

A large sculpture entitled *The Lulu Fountain* is surrounded by plants and the small fountain helps to keep the plants moist. This attic studio has a glass ceiling with peeling white paint, the floor was painted in a white preparation that is used for the white lines down the middle of roads, and the glazing bars, sills and transoms are in gloss white. Colour is supplied in the works of art and the plants.

This is a magical place.

Michael purchases the plants. Five years ago

they arrived small and contained but the passage of time has transformed them into huge growths. An ivy given as a present by Barbara Hulanicki cascades over the balcony area and a *Monstera delicosa* hangs its innumerable roots and leaves over the pediment surmounted by two huge white swans which were used to pull the 1985 Alternative Miss World throne. As some of the plants come into flower they are moved to prominent positions in the studio from the garden preparation and storage area on the north side. Thus pots of white madonna lilies fill the studio with their aroma in early July, a bowl of miniature violets in March and scented jasmine in February.

Large plain terracotta pots are used mostly as containers. The forty-foot 'window box' on the east terrace is made of old Metal Box light fittings painted black – they come in six-foot sections and have been bolted together. This year they contain a variegated ivy, pinks and white alyssum. In the Royal Wedding year, 1981, they were filled with red, white and blue flowers. Orange and pink was our Indian year! This terrace is full of old-fashioned roses such as pale pink Aga Khan and eventually they will be trained over a pergola structure. The south terrace houses the summer overspill from the glasshouse, pineapple and orange trees for instance, which are returned inside during the winter. Forsythia, a fig tree, a New Zealand flax plant and a bed of orange roses fills the terrace.

Looking out onto the west terrace are fruit-bearing shrubs, pear trees, blackcurrant, red-currant, and a morello cherry tree. A vine slowly covers the windows, small ornamental trees, a Christmas tree, red maple, flowering plum and azaleas fill the west space.

Watering is a long process and during the summer months has to be carried out daily. The self-watering system installed as an experiment on the terraces has been abandoned.

I grew up amongst a large family – four brothers and a sister in the small Cotswold market town of Witney. My first memory of the garden was tending a small six-foot strip that I filled with blue delphiniums. Later I spent many happy hours

Andrew Logan at work in his glass eyrie.

planting, building a compost box, deep digging to create a rose bed and generally 'improving' the place.

Inspiration for the garden came from a children's annual comic book. It was of a character that knocked down a wall and mowed through a secret garden with a lawnmower that went berserk and then resurrected the same wall. Of course the amount of bricks to build such a wonder was impossible but the strong image of creating beauty from destruction remained in my mind. This I put to test when I rebuilt a secret garden for a spinster next-door neighbour where there were high walls and the ground was overgrown with rampant roses. I cleaned everything up, laid the familiar winding path, and it was from then my love of plants flourished. It continued when I started to create objects in my last year as an architectural student in 1968. I created a huge daffodil light in an environment in my digs in Oxford. The floor, bed and part of myself were covered in artificial grass and the walls and ceiling were painted with sky and clouds. I even had an outfit to match.

Thus for my first exhibition 'Ten Sitting Rooms' at the ICA in 1970 I built a garden inside a city. Here there was a waterfall, a hillock, a winding path, cotton wool clouds and huge snakes' head fritillaries and a life-size latex sleeping horse acted as the settee all within the small space.

Plant imagery continued strongly in my work and culminated in the sculpture garden commissioned by Barbara Hulanicki for the Roof Garden at Biba, her London store, in 1975. This was of huge black and red fibreglass roses, irises, white lilies and ivy and real flowers were planted underneath these sculptures too, with the idea being the real flowers would eventually cover the sculptures. The scheme was planned for many years ahead, but alas, with the demise of the emporium, the property company who took over the place wilfully destroyed the sculptures.

Even though I still use plant imagery a lot in my work, that incident proved to be a turning point. My secret garden was destroyed. I felt a disgust towards humanity and its ugly attitude to objects

of beauty. It was a time of personal crisis, followed by a fire and several burglaries. It took some time for me to abstract myself and put everything into an historical context: The solution is to keep building.

Portraiture is my new departure. Even this includes flowers. I have just completed portraits of mother and father; the image of a rosebush is incorporated into the painting of my mother since roses are her favourite flowers.

I feel very privileged to be able to work alongside plants and flowers in the glasshouse and it is a reminder to me of the message to humanity. Tend the earth and it will produce bounteous things.

Thank you.

At home amongst Andrew Logan's sculpture, favourite plants including a contingent of ornamental cabbages.

MARY KEEN

Mary Keen writes a regular gardening column for a London newspaper, is a contributor to various leading magazines and sits on the National Trust Gardens' Panel. Her first book on the subject of garden borders will be published shortly. She is married with four children and lives in an early nineteenth-century rectory in Berkshire.

I WISH I had a conservatory. I'd like one with a tinkling fountain and rattan chairs where the smell of lilies and daturas and jasmine hung heavy in the air and it was always warm and green in February while the rest of the world was grey. There would be a table for tea and a reclining chair and sometimes the door to the house would be left ajar so that the smell of the flowers drifted into the hall.

I do not have such a thing. What I have is a legacy of a do-it-yourself lean-to, with a glass roof, two sides of brick and half a side of glass, which was built on to the west and plainest end of the house by the people who lived here before us. Rather mean brick pillars support the roof which is not pitched steeply enough to drain properly. This means that if it rains hard a lot of the rain comes through the glass, which is prone to going green. The glass covers an area about twelve foot by ten – a serious undertaking when it comes to removing the green and no long-handled broom is ever long enough to remove every trace of moss and slime. Originally the open spaces between the brick pillars were filled by removable doors and windows, rather along the lines of those mentioned in Russian novels. They were very heavy and needed several serfs to carry them into the garage in April and back from the garage in September. The window frames were less heavy than they might have been, because they were fitted not with glass, but with polythene, the sort that goes milky when exposed to ultra-violet rays, so they were not an adornment in winter. All this to-ing and fro-ing

was very exhausting and did not seem to improve the life expectancy of the plants much nor did it ever make the conservatory a place to linger in January, because there was no question of heating such a large area when we already had a greenhouse to keep warm. And the greenhouse was a much safer place for geraniums than an unheated and dubious 'conservatory'. So the door and window routine was gradually abandoned and it was a great relief to turn the conservatory into a loggia, a place that is open to the winds but where it is lovely to sit on a summer's day. The name 'conservatory' stuck though, and it is never referred to as anything else.

The deficiencies of the structure were not the only things we had to overcome. There was nowhere to put the plants. Our predecessors in the fifties who had arranged the mean brick pillars, flat glass roof, Russian doors and windows and composition concrete floor had also provided an above ground manhole cover in the conservatory when they turned their attentions to replumbing the house. They grouped pots tastefully round this focal point, but it remained rather visible to most people's eyes, so we built a low brick wall about three foot high all round the drain, making a sort of grave-sized brick-sided bed, which was then filled with earth. On top of the manhole cover, now

The outdoor room photographed in October at breakfast-time with peacock chair and baskets of home-grown quinces and tomatoes.

hidden with a thin layer of soil, we stood an old green lead-lined copper boiler and this too was filled with earth. Some trellis went in on the back

An old wooden table is topped with slate, the floor is concrete. Plants include a francoa, left, and the succulent Echeveria glauca *from Beth Chatto. At the back are abutilon, scented-leaf geraniums, pink passion flower, a sparmannia and grey-leafed helichrysum.*

A glimpse from the back door passage which leads from kitchen to conservatory. Chairs are elderly Habitat, recently given new canvas covers.

wall to hide the pipes that emptied the bath above into the drain below, and the first plant to go into the small bed was an ordinary passion flower to give green cover to the roof and the walls in the fastest possible time. Passion flowers do this all too well, but they are not good at co-existing with other plants and in very cold winters they pack up. After the frosts of 1984 the passion flower succumbed and I decided not to renew it, but used cobaeas to fill in, while more reliable and less rampant climbers were started. The magenta sweet pea (*Lathyrus tuberosus*) and the yellow canary creeper (*Tropaeolum peregrinum*) made good stop-gap climbers at this stage too. A trachelospermum (evergreen and fragrant, but needs a sheltered place) was an obvious choice and *Clematis cirrhosa*, the early-flowering clematis from the Balearics was another. These are the only two plants which are permanent against the house wall and they are planted in the copper and in a large terracotta pot. The little trailing *Campanula isophylla* survives one winter in three, growing in the earth at the top of the brick wall, but there are always plenty of reserve plants to use from the greenhouse when the green edge to the bed fails.

The other thing which spends the whole year adorning the conservatory is a vine trained to the glass roof. In three years of growth from a position in the flower bed outside the covered area, it has furnished the back wall and now totally shades the slate table where family meals are taken in summer. This particular vine is 'Brandt' which has small purple grapes in the middle of October and grows very quickly. I now rather regret the choice of variety and wish that I had the courage to remove Brant and install instead that most delicious of all grapes, Muscat of Alexandria, which currently grows on a south-facing wall in the kitchen garden and could do with the added protection of a glass roof in winter.

During the summer months various structural plants with good leaves like the huge *Sparmannia africana*, the ferny jacaranda, variegated abutilons, scented-leaved geraniums and pale grey helichrysum all make a background for a changing display of flowers. The geranium 'Clorinda' is probably the most reliable and long flowering of these and a cutting of that planted in the copper at the end of May climbs to the top of the trellis by the end of the summer – a bright pink flower of Clorinda can be seen to the left of the hall window, still flowering at harvest festival time. Fuchsias are tucked into odd spaces and there are usually lilies and tobacco plants, or petunias and verbena depending on what is available from a stock of plants raised in the greenhouse.

Everything is grown in pots because the soil in the brick bed is not good enough to support strong growth and it is easier to change the compost in pots to suit individual plant's needs, than go to the length of changing the stuff in the bed. Standing the pots on earth rather than on a hard surface is useful in very hot weather because it keeps them moist, for the earth is thoroughly soaked and it means that watering does not have to be done so often. Once a week the hose is dragged across the lawn and the whole area is given the monsoon treatment and every evening about four cans of water are carried to the pots, which are all fed with Phostrogen once a week. Watering is one of the pleasures of summer gardening, the tobacco plants smell delicious and the flowers in the border look more mysterious than by day and in the slower cooler pace of evening there is time to enjoy the plants.

In early spring as the garden emerges, a row of auriculas in pots, trying to look like a John Morley painting, sits on the slate table. Later perhaps basil, or curious sempervivums with their everlasting icy rosettes, or the little blue daisy *Felicia amelloides* in a blue container might take a turn on the table while summer meals come and go. The conservatory is a place where people linger after breakfast or before dinner, but apart from mealtimes it tends to be somewhere where one or two of the family sit quietly and have a little rest before moving onto something else. This could have something to do with the fact that there are only four comfortable chairs and two or three perches on the low brick wall that links the pillars. It is a good place for the gardener to sit and fret about whether the summer border lined with lavender bushes really works and a good place for the cook, too hot in the kitchen where the Aga is always alight, to work at the broad beans or the peas or the blackcurrants under the shade of the vine. It is a good place altogether, not perhaps the conservatory of my dreams, but a very convincing illusion in the sunny summer months.

Looking out down part of the late summer border where lavender, Californian tree poppy and verbena grow.

ROSEMARY VEREY

Rosemary Verey is a well-known garden designer and author of books on gardening. The widow of the architectural historian David Verey, she lives in a seventeenth-century manor house in Gloucestershire.

OUR TUSCAN TEMPLE arrived here by lorry, each individual stone numbered, to be rebuilt on its new site. Now it is the most important feature in our garden.

We had seen it in 1962 standing in its original home in the grounds of Fairford Park. It was a spring morning and a rough track led us through the vanished pleasure grounds, past an elegant orangery and a small vermiculated stone building, and on through parkland to this classical temple, standing as an eye-catcher visible from afar. The house and the land, owned by the Barkers since the seventeenth century, had been bought in 1945 by the Ernest Cook Trust. Polish families were allowed to camp in Nissen huts in the park after the war; the house had been demolished in 1957 to make way for a modern school. The future of the garden buildings, at this time in need of repair, was in question – the Trust generously thought the buildings would serve a more useful purpose if they were moved to new grounds open to the public. The orangery was given to the National Trust, and the temple came to Barnsley.

I had my doubts, David had none. He knew the exact spot where he would have it re-erected, but I found it difficult to visualize such a grand building in my cottage-style garden, and was worried about the expense: could we, should we, afford to move it? Also, my reaction was that by rights this and the two other buildings ought to remain in their original homes. Now I know without a shadow of doubt who was right: the temple has stood here for

almost a quarter of a century, loved and appreciated by us and our visitors. Sometimes when I look at it I wonder how the garden would feel without it – it has become so much a part of my life.

The temple had been accustomed to a backdrop of trees, in the landscape style, so a wanderer at Fairford would see it in the distance and approach it full of romantic and poetic thoughts. Here at Barnsley it has a completely different setting, with Cotswold stone walls on three sides and a formal pool in front. Wall and temple are the same age – in fact, while William Eames was landscaping the park at Fairford, our beautiful lichen-covered wall was being built to enclose this rectory garden. It is interesting to me that the English in the latter half of the eighteenth century, though full of fashionable thoughts of landscapes and integrating their gardens with the countryside, were not completely able to throw off the tradition of enclosures and formality. So maybe after all it is not surprising that the temple feels at home inside our wall.

The only condition that the Cook Trust stipulated when they made their generous offer was that the site should be left in a tidy condition and all traces of stone cleared away. That was no problem, but a major expense was having a large single piece of stone cut to replace the main lintel, which was cracked right through and no longer able to support the heavy pediment. At first this stone stood out in its shiny newness, but now it has mellowed and is indistinguishable in colour from the rest of the façade.

A lucky event had happened several years before, when David, passing through Fairford, was just in time to rescue a beautiful Barker coat

Rosemary Verey reading at the entrance to her outdoor garden room.

of arms as workmen demolishing the house were about to send it crashing to the ground, to be shattered for ever or to make hardcore for a motorway. Instead, it was carefully lowered and David brought it back here as a thing of beauty, not knowing that a few years later it would be joined by the temple, where it is now secured to the back wall, keeping history alive, for it was the Barker family who had the money and foresight to build the mansion and employ William Eames to landscape the park.

David chose the perfect setting, and by chance and good fortune the geometry and proportions of temple and garden worked out well. About ten years earlier we had replaced a lawn with the goldfish pond. When we came to measure up, we discovered that the pond was exactly the same width as the temple. What could have been more lucky? It was as though they had been tailor-made for each other. A foot either way would have spoilt the symmetry, and four existing Irish junipers, which had marked the corners of the lawn, visually helped the building to settle into its surroundings.

The famous garden designer, the late Percy Cane, had paid us a brief visit a short while before the temple arrived, and had explained how the lay-out of the garden was all wrong; to be successful the longest distance should contain the main vista. This remark has been of great significance to me in designing the garden, and I have always tried to remember the important role vistas can play. They must have a beginning and an end, unless, of course, they stretch into infinity, as in the grand French gardens.

We were faced with problems over our vista, which was contained at both ends by the old garden wall. Often a project seems quite simple and then when you come to carry it out all sorts of difficulties reveal themselves. Remembering Percy Cane's advice, we had to open up the whole length (a hundred yards) of the view. This entailed removing a hedge, digging up the asparagus bed and moving it into the vegetable garden, and then laying a grass path. The truth then dawned on us that if we made the path at right angles to the façade of the temple, it would not be parallel to the garden wall, which had quite a considerable kink in it. Until you start measuring up, it is easy to be unaware of these oddities. With the hedge re-

moved, the lime and laburnum walks suddenly looked as though they were slipping away to the left. Compensating was the answer. The path was laid to lead directly away at right angles to the temple – it had to be – but was widened as it went

A composition of furniture, plants and objects within the temple, the chairs designed by Charles Verey.

along. This helped but did not altogether correct the situation: the lime walk still seemed to be slithering away to the left.

I was gazing at it one day in despair, wondering

whatever could be done to make it all look right, when Nicholas Ridley walked into the garden. I presented him with my problem and in a flash he solved it for me. With his architectural talent, inherited from his grandfather, Sir Edwin Lutyens, he came out with a solution, obvious to him but which had not dawned on my more prosaic mind. The answer was to plant another row of limes in line with the new path, creating a new perspective. It worked wonders, and still does; I enjoy telling my enquiring garden visitors just how and why we have this wedge-shaped double row of lime trees.

Now I must tell you about the temple as it is today. There is a stone seat built into the back wall, sometimes with plants in pots standing on it waiting to be put outside when the weather improves. In summer I try to keep a few scented-leaved geraniums here so that visitors can pinch their leaves and enjoy the different scents. The plants change according to the seasons, but two white marble busts live their whole lives looking out onto the garden from their pedestals. In one corner is a beautiful girl with her hair braided and bunched under a bandeau and wearing large circular earrings. A young Augustus Caesar eyes her from the opposite corner. The other inhabitants are the bats, but they only come out and reveal themselves on summer nights.

A big decision we had to make was how to treat the inside walls. For quite a time we left them as rough stone, as they had been in their Fairford life, and then David decided that they should be plastered and lime-washed. This has been a success and makes the whole building much lighter. On summer days when the sun is out the interior shines up brightly, and when the sun's rays hit the water at a certain angle the reflection of the ripples on the water's surface plays on the back wall. Then there are the reflections on the water. Looking towards the temple from the far side of the pool you can see the whole of its façade repeated, and then sitting or standing in the building the blue gates are clearly mirrored. This happens best in winter when there are no water-lily leaves covering the surface. With any pond it is a point worth considering – how much surface should be kept free from vegetation?

What kind of furniture do we have? This is important from the sitting and the visual point of view. Ours is a bit of a mixture. There are six chairs, two tables and a bench. The bench is hard and uncomfortable, but as it is in the central position people make straight for it. It is a prettily designed iron seat, typical garden furniture to withstand the weather. If we are having a party here I spread cushions along it. Two other metal chairs look as though they are hard, but in reality the moment you sit on them you sink, rather surprisingly, just as you do when you sit on a half-filled air cushion, for the seat is made of narrow strips of flexible metal. There is a pair of wooden Chinese Chippendale pattern armchairs made by my son Charles, solid and very comfortable. During the summer these will often be carried out and put under a tree, somewhere with a good view or in a private place. The tables are three-legged 'Britannia' tables with an iron base and a marble top. All the furniture is painted white.

Looking back at our diaries, I am amazed at how slow we were at doing things. The temple came here in 1962, the laburnum tunnel, a silver wedding present from my brother, was planted in 1964, the grass walk happened four years later. Another four years were to elapse before the fountain arrived as an important focal point.

What should this be? The stone sculptor, Simon Verity, his wife Judith and their children had a picnic tea with us, sitting at the end of the grass walk. Simon had brought sketches and pieces of plasticine. Quickly we discarded the idea of a grand Trevi fountain, but fountain it must be to incorporate the sound and movement of water at this end of the garden. It should be both audible and visible from the temple, in no way grand but reflecting the essence of our life here in the Cotswolds. David had studied and written about the beautiful churches built by the wool merchants, whose wealth had been based on the flourishing wool trade with Italy in Renaissance times. Cotswold sheep, the source of their riches, are the main theme of the fountain. Then there were the horses which had been involved in our lives, so horses' heads and our initials were included. Simon came up with the idea of frogs spouting jets of water onto a flat stone – this would create the water sound. The stone is spangled Purbeck, the fossils in it looking like the wool of the Cotswold rams. The base on which they stand and the frogs are of Hornton stone, which when wet becomes the colour of lead.

The temple has been the making of the garden. It is a striking focal point seen from the fountain, the view would be unexciting without it; with it there is a feeling of satisfaction and completion. You are led towards it.

Then it is a place to sit quietly, to think, to read, to talk. It faces south-west, so gets full sun from midday right through until the evening. If friends call I will often take them there. In each season it has a different mood. In winter I will probably only stand inside, enjoying the view, thinking about the planting in the surrounding pond garden. Things have grown up well here over the years and there are satisfactory evergreens: a marvellous Goldheart ivy rambling through the old quince tree, a rosemary climbing a wall. An Irish ivy with a huge leaf has made a hefty mound and a self-sown yew, now four feet high, will one day make an exciting silhouette, kept hard clipped to the wall.

I love the spring mood. The hellebores flower in profusion in February and March. The *Magnolia × soulangiana*'s buds swell and finally burst open in May, and the mass of kingcups in the narrow beds round the pond make a display as bright as the daffodils. It is a wonderful vantage point from which to watch the birds, especially the young chaffinches, goldfinches and swallows. I can sit and watch them for hours in the evenings.

Summer is quite different. The irises take over round the pond, the roses and clematis on the walls come out, and everything seems lush and full. There are magic June evenings when everything is perfect and we will have a wonderful, happy *fête champêtre* dining off the marble-topped tables. Eventually, as the sun disappears behind the trees, we light the candles and the world becomes silent. The swallows make a final dive over the water, the candles gutter in the slight breeze, the bats swoop out from the rafters, and we wonder about the people who sat in the temple a century ago.

Classic revival: the temple is seen once more, within the shadowy reflection of the pond.

DAVID MLINARIC

*David Mlinaric is an interior decorator, a consultant to the
National Trust and the Foreign and Commonwealth Office,
and studied at the Bartlett School of Architecture. He has had
his London practice for twenty-three years. With his wife
Martha and their three children he lives in a mid-nineteenth-
century redbrick studio house which is one of several in a
Chelsea street originally built for working artists.*

OUR CONSERVATORY is now the dining room
and we call it the 'New Room' because we
had a very tight working and living arrangement here until five years ago when the small
backyard was added into the house.

Since then we have changed several of the rooms
within the house around. My office is now elsewhere, so we have moved our bedroom from
downstairs into the gallery overlooking the studio
where I used to work. Altogether the house has
become less crowded and what we now have in it is
a distillation of our favourite possessions.

Originally I designed the conservatory as a
place for Martha, somewhere she could sit, read,
play records and do her sewing. It used to serve
other purposes, in that it became a small sitting
room for everyone, as well as the children's
playroom, a place for watching television and
holding business meetings. Now, with the kitchen
next door, it is where we eat, although as a family
we tend to have breakfast in different places and at
different times. It works well as a room for all
seasons and as we are in London this Christmas we
have decorated the room; it lends itself well to the
style of a German Christmas with ivy, rather
heavy and dark with swags of other evergreen –
very much the style that Prince Albert brought to
England in Victorian times. In contrast to all this
winter green, on spring and summer days when
both sets of double french doors are open on the
short axis and the place feels light and airy, there is
a feeling of sitting in a glass tent.

Other than for specific occasions, there is little in
the way of plants in the New Room during our
everyday life. We came to the conclusion the room
was for the plants or for us. Big plants take up a lot
of space and in London the point is to get as much
space as possible. In our early enthusiasm we put
in things like fuchsias and daisy trees, but this
meant there was not enough room for us to move
about as we wanted to. And anyway I prefer cut
flowers. Also, I do not know much technically
about plants and I do not like the effect of a room
to depend on them in ordinary decorating. The
room should work even if you have not had the
time to put the plants in.

We wanted to keep the room just as warm as the
rest of the house and the two are run on the same
heating system. I have added a dimplex radiator
to boost it because there is a great heat loss in the
conservatory in spite of double glazing. Plants do
not like central heating and we do like it. The ideal
solution is the house that, in addition to its
conservatory, has got a greenhouse from which the
plants get brought in, but this is not available to
all that many people. For instance, there was a
house I worked in where a great mimosa tree was
brought in and put into a Chinese pot. It does
mean, though, a lot of care and carrying about and
either living on a grand scale or being enthusiastic

*A skilful balance of weight, colour and tones in the interior
design of the new conservatory.*

gardeners who put gardening high on the list of priorities of what they want to do with their house.

Nicholas Johnston the architect did the structure here and together we thought it out, taking the details of a rectangular window from this house and turning it into the glazed walls of a room by repetition of the form. The conservatory windows and their timber mouldings are identical to ones in the skylight window of the studio.

The acoustics are controlled by the sisal matting on the floor and the matting in turn helps to achieve the feeling of a room more inside than out. When you build a conservatory it is important to decide the balance you want between an inside room and one outside. A stone or brick floor would have been too cold here. As the room was intended for Martha it has been done in pastel colours and deliberately soft in effect as opposed to the masculine atmosphere of the studio, which has dark green painted woodwork and eighteenth- and nineteenth-century furniture. I chose French provincial furniture because I think it is appropriate for semi-outdoors and I thought more formal furniture and polished timber would look out of place. We began by buying a set of chairs with fretted, cut out backs because they look like halfway garden furniture and we painted these grey. Then we got the plain nineteenth-century table and next we added the French cupboard which was in one of the guest rooms at Thorpe, which was our house in the country, and it is handy for my son Max's clothes. This in turn gave rise to the idea of the French buffet sideboard. The brick walls are washed pink. The lighting is literally just one lamp which came from Stephen Long's shop and on the wall two half-lanterns which were copied from one Piers de Westenholz found in France. Outside, there are two spotlights on sticks for the flower-bed, which, when lit, are screened by leaves and with the addition of candlelight inside, make soft lighting at dinner. Then, as far as details are concerned, there is a group of watercolours painted by Louisa Parrish which record her own rooms in the nineteenth century and I bought these pictures and had them

---

A pig in the middle of leaves takes a view of an outside world beyond the glass.

Christmas Day, complete with poinsettia and pudding shows how effective the room is as a place for all seasons.

framed up for the conservatory specifically. The china we use goes well, with its pale colours on a white background, but this is entirely by coincidence since it was a wedding present.

The room is now a transformation from what used to be a rather damp and gloomy backyard and, if a back yard is all you have, then I think it is much nicer to have a conservatory which gives the

illusion of being sunny. The tall London plane trees and sycamores in the gardens round about us all contribute to an atmosphere of ground-level privacy and add an interesting feeling of urban density – rather in the way that Arab towns make their houses live away from the street and not frontwards. We still grow plants, but they are outside in a narrow bed between the New Room and the garden wall. They grow close enough to the glass to make us feel they are almost in the room and because they are in fresh air they flourish naturally. The planting is mostly evergreen and uncomplicated, such as *Mahonia japonica*, viburnum, honeysuckle and berberis, underplanted in spring with bulbs.

When my father first came to England he built a house on the Thames at Twickenham and there was a conservatory with a vine and geraniums in it. My father and my mother, my sister and myself all used to eat there in summer within the sight and sounds of the river, and so it is just possible that the desire to build a conservatory of our own stems from the pleasant memories of the childhood one. But it was really built for practical reasons: everyone likes a garden, even if it is only a window-box, and so we have combined the pleasures of indoor space, garden and sunlight.

Our room was built at a time when conservatories came back into fashion again and the reason why they are now in vogue once more makes sense. For the first fifteen years after the last war what people did with their houses was to preserve the status quo, or to do so as nearly as possible, and not many people broke new ground in having things differently. There were incredibly few houses which were 'decorated' as we speak about them now. It was not until the mid-1960s that a lot of people became excited about decoration and this new enthusiasm, combined with the perennial British passion for gardening, I think has led to the revival of the conservatory.

David Mlinaric in his New Room, photographed from the exterior, east side of the building.

LADY MARY RUSSELL

*Lady Mary Russell, the only daughter of the Earl of
Haddington, is married to David Russell who is the chairman
of an advertising agency. They live at Combe Manor, a
seventeenth-century redbrick house on the Wiltshire Downs.*

C17 GAZEBO REPUTED TO HAVE BEEN BUILT BY CHARLES II FOR NELL GWYNN stated the particulars beneath a rather faded photograph which showed an enchanting brick summer-house, the old manor house behind, and the Downs in the distance. The picture in *Country Life* was irresistible. A friend who knew the property well came to lunch a few days later and said it was fascinating, but very run down. I went with David to view it the following Sunday; it was a golden October afternoon and we walked through the neglected garden, climbing up the steep rise to where the gazebo stood in the angle of the walls. The view all around the bowl of the Downs was timeless and lonely. We knew at once that we wanted to live here and we were lucky enough to achieve our aim shortly afterwards.

The gazebo fulfils a long buried wish. When I was a child I lived in Mellerstain, a big house in Scotland, and my favourite place to spend as much time as possible was a thatched cottage, originally a lodge or toll house, situated a few hundred yards from the main house. One entered into a secret world through a wrought-iron gate. There was a lovely garden surrounding the cottage, many paths winding in and out of the clipped box hedges, lawns on which to picnic in fine weather, but the best time was when it rained or was cold, and my nanny and I would light the fire in the grate in the front room and we would cook eggs and bacon and toast our bread before the embers. Ever since then I have loved the idea of a secret,

On the path from the gazebo to the house with the abundant pink Céleste in the foreground left.

private place within one's own park or garden.

So, after the house had been restored, we moved in and presently turned our attention to the gazebo. First of all we removed a very ugly staircase which led up to the doorway, successfully obscuring the finer details of the original brickwork, the pilasters with their capitals and a curious design like a pepper pot with an enlarged knob on the top, which seems to have no coherence with the rest of the architecture yet can be found in repetition on one of the outside walls of the house. We introduced a simple wrought-iron spiral staircase, which leads from the cell-like room on the ground floor into the upper square panelled room with its sash windows on three sides and matching door on the fourth. The panelling, shutters and cornice were carefully cleaned and painted in soft off-whites, the old oak floorboards had sadly rotted and had to be replaced, cushions were fitted to the window seats, rush matting laid, a round oak pedestal table brought to hold flowers, books and magazines, and more recently, a wicker table and chairs. We added a wooden balustraded balcony rising from a brick and flint platform and lastly, the missing ball finial was restored to its rightful place on the peak of the roof. At first it all looked a little bit too new and self-conscious but the climate very soon mellowed the paintwork, the floor and the balcony bleached and the place became comfortable and peaceful.

During the reign of Charles II the Manor House was occupied by a gentleman by the name of Gabriel Whistler, who now lies buried in the little churchyard beside the house. This Gabriel was an officer in the King's army and is known to have been a personal friend of Charles, so it is possible

Detail of the painted seventeenth-century panelling in the upper room of the gazebo. On the windowseat are cushions covered in green and white patterned cotton by Combe Manor Fabrics.

that the King may well have visited his friend to join in hunting the deer over the Downs. I like to think of Nell Gwynn waiting for their return from the chase, perhaps leaning from the window of the gazebo with a basket of oranges to refresh the King

after the rigours of the day's sport! That is if this cockney 'lady' could have stood 'the tingling silence' of the countryside, so far from the sound of Bow Bells.

There is another story, concerning this same period of history, which was told to some neighbours of ours by an old gentleman who lived close by. He had a friend staying with him who was an acquaintance of the then occupiers of the Manor, and he decided to drive over and call on them. As he came round the curve of the drive he was

surprised to see figures passing the lighted windows and moving about on the grass in front of the house. Not wishing to intrude upon this gathering, he retreated to the nearest village and went into the pub. Getting into conversation with the locals he told of his visit, and as he described the figures he had seen he realized that these people had been dressed in costumes of the Restoration period. The locals were astonished to hear of these goings on, especially as the occupants were known to be away on holiday.

A yellow Golden Showers rose festoons the wooden balcony on which stand Lady Mary and her two daughters, Miss Mariana Russell (left) and Lady Chandos (centre). Rosa moyesii grows against the flint and brick garden wall into which the gazebo is set at an angle.

But, to return to the present. In order to enhance the feeling of mystery and romance which surrounds the gazebo, I have tried to make the garden approach rather wild and secret. Fortu-

67

nately there were several old plum, damson and apple trees up which to train a profusion of roses. Kiftsgate, The Garland, Wedding Day and an old pale pink rose, a gift from a friend, which has so far proved unidentifiable. There are big clumps of Nevada, and Constance Spry, the latter has grown so huge that she is starting to climb into a conveniently close laburnum. There are also some of the old-fashioned roses, Céleste, Mme Le Gras de St Germain, Commandant Beaurepaire, the old York and Lancaster roses and others, growing amongst the long grass where cowslips and primroses are being encouraged but remain reluctant. There is a choice of routes by which to reach the gazebo; you may either wind your way under the branches of the cherry tree and past the weeping silver pear (*Pyrus salicifolia* 'Pendula'), avoid being caught by the arching sprays of the roses and arrive at the doorway below the 1667 date brick; or you may wander to your right past an island bed crammed with lilac, roses, Céleste again, Cerise Bouquet, Aloha, The Fairy, Ballerina, The Wife of Bath and other plants such as hostas and the ubiquitous *Alchemilla mollis*, past a young beech tree and double back through the gap in the old yew hedge which leads you into the Walk between the old brick and flint wall on your right and the yew hedge on your left. Here I have planted several shrubs of that lovely old striped Rosa Mundi rose against the hedge and some old moss roses and a moyesii on the side of the wall. And so you stand below the balcony where Golden Showers climbs, but here I have a failure on my hands, since all my attempts to coax honeysuckle and clematis up the pillars have so far met with no success.

Our gazebo is the place that we bring our friends to for a drink in summer when the sun is setting or coffee after dinner, a place for children to study for their dreadful exams, a place to retreat to in times of sorrow, a place where one day a daughter may receive a proposal of marriage, but best of all, a place to read or write in or just to sit, think and dream and gaze at the view which remains so unchanging, reassuring and lovely.

The upper floor of the garden house with a view of the white Arab mare grazing in the paddock.

NICOLA BAYLEY

*Nicola Bayley is an illustrator of best-selling children's books
and a graduate of St Martin's School of Art. She is married to
John Hilton who is a barrister and they live with their young
son Felix in a Victorian terraced house in London,
close to Hampstead Heath.*

THE CONSERVATORY joins the dining room to the kitchen so it is used a great deal as a passage, but it has enough entertaining things in it to merit being called a playroom or music room as well as a room for plants.

We have a large ninety-foot garden so the conservatory is not relied upon for greenness. In fact, unusually for London, you can look one way through the dining room windows and in the other direction through the conservatory windows and see nothing but trees, not a scrap of house. My husband John planted mature silver birch and western hemlock as well as eucalyptus and a fast-growing false acacia (*Robinia pseudoacacia* 'Frisia') at the end of the garden to block out the warehouse on the other side of the wall, so it is only at night when work continues and the lights are on that we are aware of the building, and then it takes on a romantic air like a Fellini cardboard liner with distant poops and dongs as messages are relayed.

The room is tranquil but never completely quiet, the humidifier hisses and lots of clocks tick but we are far enough from the main road to be spared the sound of traffic. In the spring mating frogs croak and toads chirp, there is a family of shouting crows and the strange cry of a cockatiel next door. Perhaps the best sound is the thud as Bella drops onto the glass roof from the window above. It is an enchanting view of a cat and when she settles there is nothing lovelier than her flat furry bottom and fat paws seen from beneath.

It is a good place for writing letters and occasionally I work there but the light is almost too penetrating for that because of all the glass, although there is a blind like a sail to draw across

for relief. The most frequent and important activity which takes place in this garden room is playing the pianola. We inherited it with a lot of rolls from an aunt in Wales so now we can hear live renderings of transposed Beethoven symphonies or Wagner overtures. Chopin, Schumann and Schubert can be played at invigorating speed according to which knob you press and what mood you are in. Most popular requests are *Softly Awakes My Heart* and *Killarney* although *Harlequin* is a particular favourite as it has the words printed beside the tiny wind holes with a splendid verse which begins:

> Harlequin's weary
> Harlequin's grey
> Oh! it is dreary
> Making folk gay.

This is called a song roll and the words are by Comfort Parry. For a particular treat and when John is feeling strong we get out *The Hungarian Rhapsody* by Lizst, the largest roll in the collection; unfortunately we cannot share the pedalling as I find it impossible to squeeze more than four notes out despite hanging onto the furniture, both to get a purchase and avoid travelling backwards into the kitchen.

The nineteenth-century stove came from Belgium and until recently was very black inside, but

---

The conservatory, seen here from the doorway to the kitchen, has a cream coloured canvas blind to soften the sunlight. On top of the pianola is a ceramic bust of Queen Victoria.

it is clean now because Felix uses it for a giant 'Activity Centre' as toy people call them. Nuts, unwrapped cracker hats and a selection of dead coffee percolator parts are kept inside, sorted and moved about. He also keeps teaspoons in there for digging in pots and does some small-scale gardening, a ritual shake for the papyrus and a tweak for the solitary orange. The big bread-making bowls live beneath the stove. The Japanese toad on top was probably kept in a garden once and is made

Bella the tabby cat who is the model for many of Nicola Bayley's published illustrations.

from a mixture of lead and bronze. Toes and eyebrows which were missing, I fashioned in plasticine, pitted and painted grey.

The dining room with view through to the garden room. Sir William Hamilton's Etruscan views which are hung on the left-hand wall determined the terracotta paint for the walls. A painting of St Denis, patron saint of Paris, dominates the room.

The conservatory is a small room so there is only space for two pictures, a green river scene with a hole in it which John saved from his grandfather's gothick garden house; the other is of a simple hound which is almost hidden by leaves. Fresh or dried flowers can be put in the halved tureen lid hung on the wall and we keep big vases on the windowsill. Her Majesty Queen Victoria looks down from the pianola and a very thin wooden peg man sits on the windows. The floor of the conservatory is paved with Amtico tiles with a small Turkish carpet on top, which can prove hazardous for speeding cats. John put the columns in; they came from a house being demolished in Yorkshire.

The welcoming atmosphere of the day is continued at night as the lamps are left on permanently so there is always a reassuring warmth to be found. It is lovely to look back at from the bottom of the garden in the dark. A Venetian chandelier in the dining room is just visible framed by the columns.

The conservatory is mostly used for music, contemplation and mooning; gardening is sporadic and the only crop is a pot of basil. My contribution is mainly to remember to water certain plants frequently and others not. The huge papyrus we grew from a cutting drinks gallons of water and is a handy place for emptying hot-water bottles in winter. It must be happy despite not living in the Nile as it tumbles out of its pot with new shoots and occasionally has grassy flowerings from the top of its stalks. We leave the dead leaves in place because they turn a pleasing parchment colour. Some plants are permanent like the *Jasminum azoricum*, the *Hedera colchica* (Persian Ivy) and the *Philodendron erubescens* which sit on a raised triangular bed filled with gravel that is kept damp. There used to be a vast hoya spread about the walls and ceiling but it died, so we are trying again with a small hanging pot of it in order to retain the heady scent given by the waxy flowers. A spindly geranium adds a pungent whiff, but best of all are the lilies we bring in during June and July. *Lilium longiflorum* 'Holland's Glory' and 'Black Dragon' look ravishing and almost give you a headache with their extravagant scent, the only drawback being the rude orange stain made by their stamens as you brush past.

The wonderful thing about having a garden is we can bring whatever we like the look of into the conservatory for a while. At the moment there is a self-seeded oak and having it in the house makes you look much more closely at the shapely leaves. To fill in a gap made by the death of a leggy stephanotis we brought in a big pot of variegated ivy and unfortunately we brought an extensive ants' nest with it. There are surprisingly few horrid things to deal with in the conservatory and perhaps the worst was a plague of rolled-up leaves with worms inside. The other scourge is a mysterious one and causes a very sticky floor beneath certain plants and a sugary deposit on their leaves. It may be connected with the flat blistery blight which attaches itself to stems, stalks and leaves and has to be kept under control with a methylated spirit and water scrub.

The conservatory also has a very particular use at Christmas. We hang two old green lengths of silk from a bamboo pole wedged between the pillars so that they can be drawn apart like curtains and then John gives a performance of magic for assembled relations and friends in the darkened dining room. Arc lights blaze and John does his tricks; some he inherited from his grandfather, others are from a Brighton antique shop and the less rarefied ones are from joke shops. Sometimes he wears an old cloth-of-gold robe with a gold Tibetan hat, otherwise it is classic black enlivened by false noses, ears and silly spectacles. The larger props and changes of clothes are kept out of sight in the kitchen. Sometimes a quick run out of the kitchen door, into the garden, through to the hall and back into the dining room unobserved gives everyone a fright. The space really lends itself to performance and exhibition even without the help of curtains. Sometimes I imagine it as a completely bare area where a single object could be placed for admiration, then changed for another. If the Victoria and Albert Museum could be persuaded to part with the enormous marble bust of Charles II by Honore Pelle which sits half way up their right-hand staircase, deeply incised and standing six foot high from wig to regalia, I would begin clearing the conservatory immediately.

Mr and Mrs John Hilton and their son Felix by the temple at the foot of their London garden.

PRINCESS NICHOLAS VON PREUSSEN

*Princess Nicholas von Preussen is the daughter of Lord and
Lady Mancroft. She lives with her husband Prince Nicholas,
a direct descendant of Queen Victoria, and their two small
daughters in an eighteenth-century house in Somerset.*

I DO NOT get much joy from the conservatory in the winter. It is grey and cold – quite still except for the fountain that valiantly tinkles into the pond, even though most of its holes are blocked by the debris of winter. The floor is scattered with old leaves and petals. We are often away and so I cannot imagine how we will ever find enough time and skill to get it looking and smelling as it does in the summer.

I am as gloomy as this every winter. I put my head around the door, withdraw quickly into the warmth of the dining room, and despair. I am quite wrong to do so.

By the end of March, this desolate place will look pristine, swept and polished, pruned and cut back in readiness for another long summer when the conservatory becomes a sitting room. Green noses will begin to poke their way through the earth, new shoots will have sprouted, and on the first warm morning, the popping of corks and the sound of voices will be heard again.

This immense conservatory was built in 1876 when a Victorian colonel owned our Georgian house. It is an unusual, but nonetheless striking, crescent shape, seventy feet long and eighteen feet wide. There are windows and a flower bed on either side and doors at each end. At the southern end is a dome with three niches and a pond beneath.

The conservatory curves towards the south-west and is bathed in sun almost all day. Mornings are always chilly, but on a cloudless day it can be intolerably hot by lunchtime.

---

*Soaring arch at the north end where the conservatory leads
on the right to the nursery garden for the children.*

We noticed the conservatory the first time we came to see the house shortly after we were married six years ago. It was a beautiful June afternoon and as we walked up the garden towards the house, my husband said, 'Victoria, look at that. Of course, we have to rebuild it.' The conservatory was not in its prime. The dome and its rounded walls were near to collapse, such was the pressure of the earth of the bank behind. The windows and doors were non-existant and there was no glass at all. All that remained was the stonework, the iron frame of the roof and most of the floor. It looked like the rusting carcass of a whale.

And so we re-built it. It took five months. We found a blacksmith to repair the ironwork of the roof – outside, the cresting along the central join and inside, the huge windows that open on hinges manoeuvred by chains and ropes which secure onto cleats between the windows. We ripped the nettles from the pond and the ivy from the dome. For the pond, the stonemason built a new surround, and edges for the flower beds. We installed new wooden doors and window frames. The floor we thought best not to touch, as although the rain and frost had destroyed parts of it, we considered the original Victorian tiles looked better than anything with which we might replace them. The cloakroom at the north end, with its shiny black and white tiles, we left as we found, in good repair. The elegant stone arch supported by a column on each side fortunately remained intact.

Obviously, when this glass room was built there was no doubt in the owner's mind that it should be heated. It must have been filled with the most exotic plants. However, we realized that, for us,

Close-ups of the Ham stone capitals at the entrance to the north front of the conservatory balustrade (ABOVE), *and beautifully ordered detail within* (RIGHT).

this would simply not be possible, so we removed the two massive pipes that ran down each side of the building and began to plan our cold house.

With the help of my mother, a very knowledgeable gardener with a talent for looking to a garden's future, we chose plants that would not only be happy in a normal garden, but also thrive (perhaps even more happily) in a covered garden. For, although the glass does give some protection, and enables the slightest glimmer of sun to boost the temperature, the conservatory does also catch the frost, so the plants must be hardy.

I have to say I am not a great gardener, although I love the idea of it. I memorize a few names each year in order to impress my friends. I could probably write a handbook on 'How to bluff your way through gardening'. But I do know what I like, and, equally important, what I don't like.

With the invaluable help of Trevor, a man who

An aspect of the conservatory includes the tall alcove, pond and an original Victorian cast-iron jardinière (LEFT).

can skilfully turn his hand to anything, we planted the clematis, the passion flower Constance Elliott, the honeysuckles, the roses and the plumbagos. I mainly gave advice (unwelcomed) and tried hard to memorize and visualize the plants and how they would look.

They look wonderful. The *Rosa banksiae* 'Lutea' is a mass of perfect little buttons and grows facing south between two windows on the north wall, entangled with the yellow Mermaid rose, the *Jasminum officinale* and *Jasminum humile revolutum*. The fluffy *Clematis tangutica* climbs up and over the door which opens onto the garden and takes liberties by spreading out of one window and in through another.

Amongst the spring bulbs and the summer lilies, white regale, pink spotted martagon and orange henryi, grow wild strawberries in abundance. The verbena and rosemary bushes are surrounded by hostas of all varieties. To the arch clings a nameless, ancient pink rose, a wonderful legacy for it is the only plant to survive the many years of neglect, and in various pots and urns grow hydrangeas, ginger and lilies. Beneath the rose a hellebore brought from Robert Graves' garden in Majorca flourishes.

I bought Lloyd-loom furniture, made in the fifties, from junk shops and had it sprayed British Racing green. My mother-in-law made us a dozen patchwork cushions for the chairs, which look wonderful amongst the plants. Her tiny stitches are as neat as those of any mouse that helped the Tailor of Gloucester in his time of need.

By the pond stands a circular four-tiered *jardinière* made from two original ones that were in rusty pieces on the floor. It is covered in variegated ivies and an ivy-leaved geranium with purply blue flowers which began as a cutting from Majorca.

The conservatory is a summer room – our summer dining room too. In May we had a ball for my husband's birthday and the conservatory was decorated with hanging baskets of *Alchemilla mollis*, lilies and carnations sprayed pale mauve. In the day we put up a huge calico umbrella which shades the entire table, a necessity as the children

A view of the curved roof and dome of the conservatory – an addition to the original house.

particularly find it uncomfortable to eat when it is too hot or too bright. We light it with spot lights, high up on the stonework on either side. At night we dine there, and have dimmed lights with candles and crystal hurricane lamps on the table added to the lights of the dining room through which we carry 'les spécialitées de la maison'.

Even with a few people talking, the noise is incredible, and you can hear very little when the fountain is working. A somewhat eccentric peer of the realm known to me for some thirty years, sits often in the conservatory of a morning with the newspapers and a glass of Guinness in hand. He claims the sound of the fountain, although pretty, is most unsatisfactory as it causes him to take a fair bit of exercise walking to and from the small room at the far end.

Of course, Nanny is hysterical about the children and the pond. However, the only person who has ever fallen in is my dachshund Lily. Her enthusiasm for the sport of catching goldfish has always been discouraged, but she will not listen, and on several occasions she has plummeted over the edge into the lily leaves and weeds. The children throw themselves about in appreciation of this display and beg for a repeat performance, but I lead her quickly away, as I know she could never climb out un-aided.

Butterflies and birds, thrushes, wrens, and crowds of sparrows are constantly in and out of the conservatory, especially in the evenings, when we water. But, contrary to the observation of the Duke of Wellington to Queen Victoria in the Crystal Palace, we can manage without sparrow hawks.

Part of the Latin inscription inside the dome, roughly translated, says: 'Farewell to the labours of the city, farewell henceforth to mental obstacles which had been placed before me ...' Some summer nights, the surrounding valleys of the Blackmore Vale are heavy with mist and the scent of jasmine and lilies fills the air. Sitting in the conservatory surrounded by the garden, I find it quite easy to bid any labour or obstacle farewell.

A cast-iron nineteenth century Irish urn marked Spencer of Dublin. In the background a canvas and wood umbrella covers a table on which are placed crystal hurricane lamps.

LORD RAGLAN

The fifth Lord Raglan is the great-great-grandson of Lord Fitzroy Somerset, formerly Military Secretary to the Duke of Wellington, and later Commander-in-Chief of the British Army during the Crimean War. Lord Raglan is a farmer, the patron of The Raglan Baroque Players and Singers and drives and maintains a Bugatti racing car. The family home is Cefntilla, a stone Jacobean house in Monmouthshire.

THIS PLACE is named the Sun Room because it is short to say and is too small to be dignified by the name conservatory. I made the addition in 1971 since the house is fairly dark inside and from any other room you sit in it is difficult with comfort to look directly onto the garden.

Architects tend to think they are very original people, but I believe that in truth they are subject to every fashion that blows. This house was designed by those who went to Italy on the Grand Tour in the seventeenth century, and took up the idea of facing their houses north away from the sun, planting a dark curtain of green to keep the sun off the south side. The house was built in 1615, but was rehabilitated in the 1850s, by which time the fashion had come round again. So when Matthew Digby Wyatt of the architect family, who married a local Usk girl and worked on several houses in the vicinity, came to work on Cefntilla in the middle of the last century, he compounded what the Jacobeans had done. He extended the house upon the same principle, committing all the offices, passages and staircases, you name it, to the south front. Otherwise he did a difficult job well.

I think the north-facing house was a thoughtless architectural fad in the same way nowadays with piazzas, which have been uncritically imported,

The folding campaign chair was used by an earlier Lord Raglan during the Crimean War. A bust of the Duke of Wellington guards the doorway to the study.

although ideal in Naples. To plant ideas such as these into an inimical ambiance does not make sense to my mind, but a warm glasshouse does, and I would love to have grown up and found a pretty Victorian conservatory here. However, unlike my parents who enjoyed gardening, my grandmother disliked the country, so my grandparents, who could have built one, lived here very little.

My family are scions of the Dukes of Beaufort whose ancestors used to live at Raglan Castle. When my great-great-grandfather was made a peer, his friends declared that he should now have a country house. When he protested that he could not afford one, they clubbed together to buy him one and most of them later subscribed again to a Raglan Memorial Fund with which the then derelict Cefntilla was bought as the closest available house to Raglan. By coincidence it was the house used by Sir Thomas Fairfax as his headquarters during the siege of the castle in the Civil War.

The house has remained much the same for the last hundred and thirty years. As well as adding the Sun Room I have done away with some Victorian passage walls. This entailed abolishing the dining room, which was too far from the kitchen, now forty-six feet long, where we eat instead. The glass room is a good place for drinks and talk. I use it too for gatherings with, say, the local farmers' club or charitable functions four or five times a year, mostly during the summer, when people can spill out into the garden, for it gives

The sitting room links the conservatory through spaces which were originally filled by Jacobean windows (RIGHT).

access to the garden where a good link did not exist before.

The open spaces linking the Sun Room and the present sitting room were windows in Jacobean times, but when the Victorians invented privacy and segregation of the classes, a passage was put there instead to allow the servants to ferry back and forth between the two ends of the house. In order to build the Sun Room I demolished a gloomy guests' cloakroom and lavatory which I think had been built originally as a silver cupboard. I remember this as a child, rather musty with boots and coats when there were often people staying, sometimes for months at a time during the war, and before the concept of just the weekend.

There are trees and lawns at the front of the house with hardly a flower in sight, rather in the manner of many Scottish gardens. Here, at the back, is the rectangular Jacobean garden, and beyond it stretches the Victorian landscaping which meanders between little vistas. The two ideas make a very pleasing contrast and for agreeable walking.

The house is built right down in a hollow which is very nice on windy days but the place does not get day-long sun and is something of a frost trap. One delight of this glass room is of course the extra light and the way the heat is retained, so I use the room especially in summer and on warm days in winter. I go there at lunchtime and read the newspapers with a cup of coffee, though I rarely eat there.

Everything I have planted myself. When it was first built, I used to fiddle about in the Sun Room a lot and I would potter in it late at night, sometimes after coming back from London, but now I am content to feel that it is there and that the plants grow at will. Many things have grown there at different times, but the ones there now are really

Reflections on the glass surface of the garden room window (FAR RIGHT).

On a habitat sofa strewn with a collection of sun-faded materials Lord Raglan sits with a favourite dachshund.

stephanotis, but it keeps on growing. There is an agapanthus in a fine Victorian Doulton *jardinière*, an asparagus fern and some oak-leaved geraniums. The roots of the vine have found their own way out to the wet. Some years the plumbago flowers better than others and I could not tell you why, but it is always nice and green. Then there is a jasmine which grows vigorously regardless and which I have to keep trimmed hard back.

I feel comfortable in here surrounded by things which are mostly inexpensive and which twenty years ago would have been regarded as junk; for instance, a Minton china foot bath, which is the home of the rush. Also, there are objects of family association like my great-great-grandfather's campaign chair and then there is a wicker garden seat known as a bundler, where I remember my mother in a straw hat would sometimes recline on summer afternoons. Perhaps people would gather for tea and, in an era when children still tended to be seen but not heard, my elder sister and I would be encouraged to join our parents and their friends. From here in the Sun Room I can see the spot where trays used to be brought out, maybe with cucumber sandwiches and perhaps seed cake. Indoors at teatime the kettle had a methylated spirits burner underneath it, but not on the lawn as the flame would have been blown out.

The double-glazed walls and cork floor have turned out rather well for a modest conservatory and I have just added a pair of teak chairs by Ettore Bugatti, the car designer, which look angular but are very comfortable. From here it is just a few steps down to the path, where, if I feel energetic, I can follow further, through the gate and past the topiary to the little arboretum. When the wind blows from the south-west you can hear the wheels of industry roaring on the motorway half a mile away in the Sun Room as well as in the garden, but there is also the sound of the trees. Sometimes when it is winter, dark and cold, nothing is cosier than to sit in there and listen to the gale in the screen of oaks, passing overhead with a sound like a train.

A bugatti-blue rug and flamboyant hat lie on a wicker bundler-seat, a perfect shape for relaxation.

survivors of my régime of simply adding a quantity of water about once a week. Originally I was encouraged to have a Maréchal Niel rose as well as a muscat grape, but the rose was not suited. The amaryllis nearly all came from Woolworth and simply love it here, the sparmannia threatens to take the place over, the African rush is a continual delight and the china plant I thought was a

LADY HENDERSON

*Lady Henderson is a journalist and designer. Her husband
Nicko is a former member of the Foreign Office whose last post
was Ambassador to Washington. In London Sir Nicholas and
Lady Henderson live in a small house in Knightsbridge.*

SURELY, it was bound to happen – one day we
would have to have our own conservatory.

In Vienna, our first post after we were
married, we used to wander through Fischer
von Erlach's garden rooms in Schönbrunn and
Hildebrandt's Garden Palace for Prince Eugen,
the Lower Belvedere. We noted how the long
glazed windows threw back the rays of the sun
onto the gilt and stucco walls and painted ceilings
and we saw how the windows themselves acted as
giant picture frames for the formal garden *par-
terres* outside. In 1975, twenty-seven years and
many postings later, we were transferred to Paris.
There we lived in Pauline Borghese's silk-walled
'Love Nest' as the Hôtel de Charost was called
when the Duke of Wellington purchased it from
Napoleon's favourite sister to serve as the British
Embassy. Built in the French eighteenth-century
manner – *'entre cour et jardin'* – this small palace is
itself almost a conservatory. The mirrored walls
reflect the garden – bringing trees and flowers
right into the house and filling the rooms with sunlight. The eighteenth-century archives refer to the
rooms as being 'lit by the garden' – an advantage stressed in the 1814 original sales contract,
because light at that time meant a saving on
candles for the chandeliers and Pauline, who was
most careful with her household accounts, knew
well that this was an important selling-point for
the palace.

In 1826 Lord Granville, who was the British
Ambassador at the time, added a glazed gallery to
the embassy building. This was designed by a local
architect Luigi Visconti (who later designed
Napoleon's tomb at Les Invalides) and acted as a
link between the state dining room and the
ballroom which Pauline Borghese had added to
the eighteenth-century palace. There were over a
thousand guests at the New Year's ball given to
celebrate the new gallery, but afterwards Lady
Granville, faced with the problem of costs, wrote in
her diary: 'I cannot make my accounts come
right'. Then, as today, estimates and actual costs
for running the palace did not tally. Nicko, my
husband, and I used the glazed gallery on a variety
of occasions. We used it for lunch parties, candlelight dinners and for exhibitions. British electrical
equipment, British cheeses and indoor plants and
cut flowers flown out from England were among
the diverse products displayed in those august
surroundings. But now, let us get matters into
proportion and look at our own house in London –
almost the smallest house in Knightsbridge.

Before we embarked on our peripatetic career
we had installed a cheap conservatory at the back
of our London house. In order to link it up with the
drawing-room french window on the first floor we
added wooden railings and a wooden bridge. When
we returned, after some thirty years abroad, we
found the conservatory rusty and dejected. The
sliding door had stuck and would not shut; a
tenant had set up his washing and drying ma-
chines there; a builder had installed a hot water
tank in a voluminous bright orange cover and a
thrush had chosen to build her nest on one of the
conservatory slats. The wooden bridge and railings had rotted and were dangerous.

Not wanting to find myself in Lady Granville's

---

*Roof-top view looking down on the conservatory with the
dome of Brompton Oratory in the background.*

predicament, I searched for an inexpensive firm who would install a small but pretty conservatory and another who would make plain but good railings and stairs. After looking through magazines I came across a firm who supply solid and elegant pieces of conservatories that fit together like meccano and whose work adapted well to a drawing suggested by our architect Nicholas Johnston.

Nicko and I added decorative glass door panels and a centre panel with a design of a huge urn filled with spring flowers, which were both junk shop trophies from Matthew Townsend in St John's Wood. These had to be fitted into the original plan but they did not deter our gifted local carpenter, Mr Fenech, who put the conservatory up for us. An

The wallpaper of the study is an original hand-blocked William Morris willow pattern by Sanderson, in keeping with the garden room beyond.

efficient and helpful firm who deal in wrought iron installed the railings and steps. The minute working space meant that each feature had to fit together like a jigsaw-puzzle. Finally, to give a feeling of depth, I chose small, modern, black and white tiles for the floor and had them set into a diamond pattern.

The area is tiny but it serves as a new garden window to the small house and it gives light and room for plants and flowers. My minuscule study is now enlarged and I am provided with a perfect excuse to stop working and instead dead-head, spray or water the roof garden.

Over the years we have learnt which plants flourish best and which attract white-fly (this being the main curse of our greenhouse), but for all plants we find feeding, and in fact over-feeding, works wonders. Plumbago thrives and so does oleander; sweet-smelling mint geraniums, lemon and orange bushes do well too. Our feathery-leaved pepper tree, bought because it reminded me of the pepper trees outside my nursery window in Athens, where I lived as a child, puts out promising bright green shoots and the mimosa seems to come out in blossom when we least expect it. We have bought most of our plants from an enterprising nursery garden near our country cottage. Added to these are pots which have been given by friends. (We ask a favourite London florist to suggest this when friends wish to send us flowers.) And, of course, from time to time we buy on impulse from London nurseries with their tantalizing displays.

Nicko has a gardening time schedule and plants many bulbs in the autumn. As soon as it is grey outside his paper-whites come out. These are the amateur gardener's delight because they seem to need nothing special to feed them and come up in any kind of soil or pebbles. Nicko plants them in old jelly moulds so that they look decorative when brought into the house. His hyacinths, daffodils and tulips start life covered in earth in our country cottage garden. They are later brought up into our London conservatory as if to advance the arrival of spring.

Our conservatory of course bears no resemblance to Austrian garden palaces or the glazed gallery in the Paris Embassy, but, being our own creation and with just room for two, it gives us

infinite pleasure. Sometimes, when referring to our diplomatic career, people ask: 'Do you miss *it*?'. Depending on my mood I reply, 'What is *it*?' or just 'No!'. Because, although we have enjoyed visiting and living in palaces, they belonged to other people and were only temporary homes. Our feelings towards our tiny roof garden and the conservatory attached to our small house in London are different – it is ours and we made it.

We watch with loving interest our passion flower climbing up through the *Clematis montana* 'Rubens' and in and out of the honeysuckle on the garden wall. They are planted in big pots and need frequent feeding and watering but we follow the advice which a great friend, Frances Partridge, said her gardener had given her: 'Wait until they ask for it and then give them plenty'. We tend with care (and with nail scissors!) our clipped rosemary bushes which we brought back from Washington. After we had obtained special permission, shaken the roots free of every bit of earth, we carefully packed the two bushes in our hand luggage for the journey. Sometimes they do look homesick but soon perk up when fed and happily display their pale blue flowers. The two mosaic garden tables, made for us by artist Justin Vulliamy, give a dash of colour on the darkest winter days and almost look their best after a spell of rain when every stone shines brightly. Justin worked with Boris Anrep on projects such as the floors at the Bank of England and the National Gallery and the decoration of Westminster Cathedral. The stones he used for us were leftovers from those buildings.

It is the combination of plants, flowers and coloured stones that seems to amaze our friends and visitors – it is so unexpected. But London birds take it for granted now as they perch on the trellising, chirping with delight and greedily eyeing the promising buds and young green shoots behind the glass panels of our conservatory.

Looking back at the conservatory from the stairwell. The rolled-up roof blinds are in slatted wood.

JOHN MERTON

*John Merton is a professional painter. With his wife Penelope
he lives and works at Pound House, a house which he built
in 1959 near the village of Oare on the Wiltshire Downs.*

BUILDING garden rooms is in the family. We
were five boys and three of us spent part of
our youth in a house at Oxford which had a
Victorian conservatory. Later my brother Geoffrey built a covered pool with glass over it in his
London garden. It had a paved area around it in
which he grew house plants and there was plenty of
room for a supper party, ping-pong and a sauna
bath. My brother William built an extension to
his house in the country, elegantly eighteenth-
century in style, with high windows facing south
and some top light from industrial dome lights
hidden by a parapet wall from the outside. It had
built-in flower beds and he grew temperate plants.
There was a kitchen and it was a beautiful and
comfortable room to live in. When he moved he
built an attractive little orangery as part of the
new house where he grows bougainvillea as well as
oranges and lemons.

I have also built a garden room at Enford where
we lived before and these combined experiences
taught me what I want and how to build this one,
which is now, after seven years, well tested for sub-
tropical plants.

My ambition was to build one in which my wife
and I could enjoy living day and night and in all
seasons. I wanted her to be able to look after it
herself which she was not able to do at Enford
because our old gardener Mr Bee, who was the
nicest of people, said to her, 'Madam, when you are
away in London I am not going to look after it for
you.' He had rigid ideas about divided responsibility. Jim Russell, the landscape designer, was

*A corner of the room showing the bedroom window and
adjoining dining room.*

our mentor and produced rare and beautiful plants
for us but it is only in the last seven years that my
wife has really learned how to look after this
garden room herself.

I will describe what it looks like, but for those
who are interested in the invisible engineering
there are technical notes on the heating, cooling,
watering (rain-water), drainage, ventilation, humidity control, roof construction, blinds, awning,
fumigation and lighting.

The room is thirty-six by eighteen by eleven feet
and is built onto the south side of the house in front
of the drawing room from which it can be separated by glass sliding doors with white traditional
glazing bars.

The south wall of the house inside the garden
room is made of flint and brick and stone with cut
black flint within the pediments above the
windows. The floor is paved with graved York
stone slabs of slightly varied colour and there are
low stone walls with copings containing flower
beds along the east and south walls. At other
positions some beds drop straight into the stone
floor. There is a walled octagonal bed in the middle
of the room full of spathifyllums which have
flowered profusely every day for seven years.
South of the bed is a large area of glass from floor to
ceiling, half of which opens onto a York stone
terrace flanked by two ceramic pots from Biot in
France containing *Ceanothus thyrsiflorus*, then a
lawn sloping down to a large pond, the spoil from
which was used to raise miniature downs around
one side. Beyond is open farm land with the real
downs of the Pewsey Vale in the distance and,
typical of this part of the country, a silhouette of a
white horse made by removing the grass and
exposing the chalk below.

In the winter the bog plants around the pond, some of which are twelve feet high, die down and the view from this window, as seen from the drawing room, would be rather austere if it were not for this great clump of spathifyllum which is six foot high and six foot wide.

At the east end the garden room becomes part of the dining room, separated by sliding glass from floor to ceiling. At the west end there is a decorated eighteenth-century lead tank into which water splashes from the mouth of a lead marine monster. Looking out over this end of the room is our bedroom window.

At nine o'clock this Sunday, 26 January 1986, I opened the curtains. A low sun was lighting up brilliantly fifteen Eucharist lily flowers within three feet of the window. The drooping heads were four feet high and, sitting on the carpet, I could look up at the beautiful, rarely seen, green structure inside the lily. I rushed off to get a camera. A garden room is a paradise for flower photographers because you live with the flower and can catch her looking her best at the right age and in the best

Across the water to the south front of the house with the garden room to the left of centre.

light, at the right angle and in the best setting (there is no wind for these long exposures with a tripod). The temperature was 73°F and there was thin ice on the pond outside. By this evening it had dropped to 70°F. After lunch we read the Sunday papers sitting in rattan chairs around a green marble-topped Swedish coffee table where there is room for eight people to sit. A seven-foot high chased bronze crane stands over a three-foot Biot pot which is almost hidden by the sixteen-inch leaves of the anthurium it holds. At the other end of the sitting area, remote from the dining room is an elegant and exceedingly comfortable rattan chaise longue with springs in the base and a tilting back which I gave to my mother years ago. You can wheel it into hot sunlight near a pot of gardenias or into the shade under a stephanotis trellis. There is a delicious smell, a gentle change of air, and no noise.

The drawing room, garden room and dining room are all open to one another. A large unframed mirror nine-foot long covers that part of the dining-room wall which is opposite the east end of the garden room. A party of young were standing at the opposite end. My nephew, who is rather short-sighted, pointed towards the dining room and said, 'Who are those people over there? I have not been introduced to them.' Those people appeared to be one hundred feet away in another garden room.

After dark the general illumination is provided by forty dimmed thirty-watt lamps above the ceiling, which is a sort of transparent eiderdown. Eight lamps hang above the plants on almost invisible wires. The shades are like Chinese hats one-foot wide and they conceal clusters of two, three or four bus lamps. Their heights and positions can easily be changed to suit the flowers and leaves, and not one has failed in seven years. The visible roof structure is a white rectangular grid of narrow moulded beams. At the bottom of each beam is fixed a barely visible stainless steel wire, which supplies low voltage electricity to the hanging lamps where required. Two thin uncovered fuse wires are used both to supply and support the lamps from the beam wiring. (You cannot electrocute yourself.) An underwater lamp inside the tank is also a source of light, throwing flickering beams onto the stone wall behind the tank, water from the monster's mouth disturbing the surface and bending the light. A sheet of glass slightly below the water's surface supports oxidized copper water-lily leaves and an opening flower.

The pond area can be seen lit up at night and two underwater lamps enable very healthy ten-pound rainbow trout to be seen gliding past in the clear water. This is fun, but when a visitor sees the garden room at its best on a sunny day for the first time and enters it through the drawing room, the plants and flowers can be breathtaking. Some of the plants are seen against walls covered with rough cork bark panels closely fitted, some against the four windows, and the cork and windows share the wall space in about equal proportions. Leaves and flowers seen against the light or partly by direct light and partly transmitted can be presented at their best. Creepers are on bamboo trellises fixed to the cork wall. Stephanotis grows over a horizontal bamboo trellis nine foot high and nine wide, which can be hung vertically for pruning. Plants which do not require so much light are grown under this area. The two south windows have trees made of cork bark fitted around rigid supports upon which grow various plants. Bamboo-coloured pinoleum blinds can cover all the glass, and those blinds with flower beds below them are protected from water splash by being behind secondary windows. They are raised and lowered remotely without opening the secondary windows.

In summer an electrically-operated awning keeps the sun off the twelve feet of glass in the middle of the south wall. The glass doors are not opened much because of wind and insects getting in. We actually sit in a courtyard open only to the south and furnished with teak chairs and table and eat outside under a large umbrella, often with the younger generation including our grandchildren. But in the evening the garden room comes into its own again for us to enjoy together or as a glamorous and happy setting for a supper party.

Hidden Engineering

HEATING

The floor is a giant 'block heater' – a block of concrete more than twice as thick as is recommended by the electricity board for floor heating, partly in order to accommodate pipe work. It sits on 2-inch polyurethane insulation board itself laid over rough concrete. The screed containing the heating wires is covered with 1 inch of York stone. It is in three sections on a 3-phase supply and uses economy 7 electricity which is nearly a third of the price of day electricity but is only supplied at this price for 7 hours per night when industry does not use much. This limitation is only acceptable if the insulation of the building is much better than most greenhouses.

INSULATION

Normally the greatest heat losses are from the ceiling because hot air rises. The ceiling has five dead air spaces (the one at Enford had two). This is achieved without too much loss of light by having 40 industrial dome lights each with a double perspex skin. Below this is a lamping area and then the sort of 'transparent eiderdown' mentioned previously. This is two layers of

polythene bubble material (made for packing glass) with 1-inch hemispheres on one side and a flat surface on the other. By laying two layers one upon the other, flat to round, three dead air spaces are formed. This very light and transparent material is supported on nylon fishing gut stretched across a light wooden frame which forms the top section of the side of the visible moulded beam structure. Five almost invisible threads hold up this insulating and diffusing layer. Replacing the lamps is done by springing the light frame up and over the head of two wood screws projecting sideways out of the beams on two opposite sides. Since the lamps are well dimmed replacing them is rare.

WINDOWS

All windows are double-glazed sealed units and those with flower beds below them have secondary windows also. The satin finish aluminium frames containing the glass are set into iroko wood frames, which are unpainted.

ROOF CONSTRUCTION

The roof is constructed of deep narrow wooden beams supporting aluminium industrial dome lights with a narrow asphalt cat walk between them. Aluminium paint protects the asphalt from overheating. Two of these lights are opened by electric motors controlled by a room thermostat. A parapet wall hides the domes.

VENTILATION

Air is blown into the house through expendable filters (filthy after four months use) and past a radiator which is heated by a water heat pump in winter. (In exceptionally hot weather it is used for cooling the garden room from 90°F to 83°F.) This air passes through the drawing room and dining room into the garden room and escapes through the opening lights in the roof. Therefore if the garden room is humid the drawing room is not.

A 12-inch emergency fan hidden by a cork baffle draws air out after fumigation or if the room gets too hot when the opening lights are closed for the winter.

SHADING WINDOWS

Pinoleum blinds are remotely controlled by nylon cords passing over small stainless steel pulley blocks.

A subtle interplay of light and shadows create an exotic, peaceful atmosphere.

In quiet contemplation of the pond and huge expanse of sky, seen from the garden room after a fall of rain.

CEILING

The top of the perspex domes are painted with white emulsion paint on the south facing slope of the dome every two years (half-an-hour's work). This stops the air in the cavity above the polythene bubble material getting too hot at high noon in midsummer and melting it. A sensor in one cavity informs a meter in the control cupboard of this temperature. This top light shading is not removed in the winter but the slight loss of total daylight does not seem to affect plant growth.

WATERING

Once a day a clock switch starts two electric timers which turn two solenoid valves on and off for two different periods of minutes, during which times water flows at roof tank pressure through two $\frac{3}{4}$-inch polythene pipes within a large diameter rigid polythene sleeve bedded into the concrete floor.

The water in the tube that flows longest is for the higher plants where the water pressure is lower. Under each flower bed and at other points in the floor there are cavities through which the $\frac{3}{4}$-inch poly tube passes. Small brass nozzles are pushed into this tube with a special tool and are shaped so as to lock in. Black spaghetti tubes are fitted over these nozzles and come up through the soil where they are fitted onto controllable nozzles on pegs, which water a particular spot. The number of spaghetti tubes used depends on the size of the bed or pot. There are a number of small pots standing on the coping stone edge of the bed which require hand watering. Two flush stone lidded cavities in the floor accommodate enough coiled hose to reach all plants.

RAIN-WATER is provided from a fibre glass 2680 gallon clargester, sunk in the lawn, which is filled from the roof catchment area (approx 500 sq yds) a small roof tank calls in a pump at the clargester site to keep itself topped up. As a result of using rain-water the soil does not become chalky and the valves and nozzles do not block up. In five years it has never been less than half full.

Water from a lead marine monster splashes into a handsome eighteenth-century tank at the east end of the room.

DRAINAGE

All the beds are drained by pipe work under the floor and soil is prevented from blocking them with broken tiles supporting fibre glass mat. A separate soakaway was built to ensure that the use of Temik did not harm anything nearby.

LIGHTING

The garden room hanging lamps are bus lamps which are run off a transformer at 24 volts. I have not changed one in seven years. The supply and support wires are 30-amp fuse wire. You do not get an electric shock from touching them.

Underwater lighting in the pond is two internally silvered par lamps made for outside use. They have lasted seven years underwater with no protective cover. Fish are not electrocuted. The *underwater* lamp in the lead tank does not have a par lamp because the electrolytic action of the lead and brass in water corrodes the brass. Two bus lamps are inside a perspex cylinder.

The ends are sealed by two squares of marble held against them with two external tie rods and butyl sealant. A clear polythene tube is sealed into one end and the electric wires pass through this to above the water level where there is an air seal at the wire exit. However, the expansion of air heated by the lamps necessitates the venting of the system. One end of a fine diameter polythene tube is sealed into the end of the sleeve tube from which the wires exit, and the other is sealed into a polythene bag, which fills and empties with the same air. If this is not done the cylinder soon fills with water from the moist air in the room which condenses on the inner surfaces of the unlit cylinder.

CONTROL CUPBOARD

Hidden cork covered doors conceal watering clock switch, timers, solenoid valve filters, roof-temperature monitor, lighting dimmers, switches for sockets around the room used for fumigators, hoover, and awning, and switches for exterior lighting and pond underwater lighting.

Biot pots on paving outside are insulated and heated with a low temperature wire. If a wire fails it is indicated by a small ammeter in the drawing room hidden behind a curtain.

A close-up of exotic planting in the sub-tropical garden-room.

MARY MONTAGU

*Mary Douglas-Scott-Montagu is a third-year student
of theatrical design at the Central School of Art and Design.
Her home is at Beaulieu in Hampshire and it is at her mother's
home nearby in the New Forest that the painted
waggon garden room often rests.*

MY GARDEN ROOM is often on the move. It is a room at home in the garden, in the fields or the forest and a room that takes to the roads. For this is a showman's waggon and as a garden room it works well for every season of the year.

A showman's waggon is not to be confused with a gypsy caravan, nor for that matter are the travelling showmen to be confused with gypsies, for each have their own traditions and customs. The showmen owned and managed the touring fairgrounds, and travelled the country in their custom-built waggons, setting up their rides and amusements at the country fairs. Their living waggons had mahogany panels, engraved glass windows and mirrors, and decorated ceilings, and were much more luxurious in construction than a simple gypsy caravan.

Ours is a Burton waggon, gilded and painted deep maroon red, having been built around the turn of the century by George Orton, Sons & Spooner of Burton upon Trent. Orton was a wood carver and Spooner a coach-builder, and together they established a business which built waggons and fairground equipment, such as roundabouts and slides, for the travelling showmen. This waggon was built for George Pickard, a showman who worked around the London area, and in the frosted glass windows are engraved his initials set in shields and surrounded by a key pattern. Sub-

sequently it was purchased from the Pickard family by Bill McAlpine, but he did no work on it, and it was still in its original state when it was bought from him by my mother. In the lockers were bingo cards from the fairground days, and a pair of delicate golden dancing shoes. I wonder who had danced in them? The lamps and stove were all in good working condition, though the beautiful painted ceiling was quite black from years of smoke and dirt from the coal fires.

The showman's living waggon is well-planned, shipshape and neat with every available inch put to good use and equipped with most of the requirements needed to live a comfortable life. No space is wasted and the furniture is all built in. In the centre of one side, fitted into a recess lined with enamelled metal plates depicting daffodils, is the original Hostess stove with mantelpiece and mirror above, these hide the chimney flue which is channelled to the right to create an airing cupboard. The stove will burn either coal or peat and the waggon quickly warms up when it and the paraffin lamps are lit, and becomes snug and inviting. Opposite the stove is a cupboard with glass doors in which is displayed a fine china tea-set, belonging to my mother, with a folding table underneath. Every inch of space is utilized throughout, with seats opening up to reveal storage space beneath, and most cunning of all is the bed across the back end of the waggon, which by day is concealed by three sliding doors of cut glass mirror, but at night can be pulled out when needed to make a good size double bed. The panels surrounding the bed on three sides are painted with bunches of carnations. The crowning glory is

the ceiling, a mass of roses and clematis and intertwining passion flowers set in gilded mouldings of egg and tongue carving, which is being restored by my mother to its original state.

The waggon has been with us for about fifteen years now and has its home base at the side of my mother's house in the New Forest, under a purpose-built canopy, really not much more than a corrugated-iron lean-to, which gives protection from the worst of the winter. In summer honeysuckles, white jasmine, roses and also a grape vine

The elaborate fireplace complete with coal-fired cooking range, carved overmantel mirror and an original etched glass oil lamp.

grow all round the canopy and form a beautiful flower-filled frame for my garden room. I have made my own wine from the grapes and exhibited it at local agricultural shows. Later, in midsummer when it is really warm, the waggon is wheeled out and parked in the shade of a large oak tree.

For some years now, when my attic bedroom at the house becomes too hot, I move to the waggon. I take my radio, a few favourite books, cushions galore for the bed, and freshly picked soft fruit from the garden to nibble on. This move always seems to coincide with the flowering of the sweet peas, my favourite flowers, so I pick large bunches

hand and watch the swallows catching flies in the fading sunlight. As dusk falls the paraffin lamps are lit and cast their soft glow around the mirrored panels. It is a wonderfully romantic place in which to sleep, the cut glass mirrors reflecting the light and creating an illusion of space and mystery, and when the wind blows the waggon sways like a ship

---

A detail showing the elaborate carving. A water urn and jam tarts stand ready for tea.

Frosted glass window panels and a rag rug frame a view of the clearing with brazier and antique portable washbasin.

of them to fill the waggon with their sweet scent and subtle colours. This is a smell that always evokes many memories of time spent in my growing-up, lazing around on hot summer days in the waggon. There I am joined by the household pets: Precious the cat, Twiggy the whippet, and until recently Toyah the canary, and we make it our home. It is the most luxurious and magic escape from the mundane pressures of everday life. Here on a summer's evening I can sit on the steps with a glass of home-made elderflower wine in my at sea. Here I am truly happy and content.

Once we had a wren living in with us, and she flew in and out of the open top window in the waggon roof and made a nest on the mantle over the stove mirror. As can be expected, she left a delightful pattern of messes over everything so was not too popular a visitor. The waggon is a haven for all sorts of small wild creatures, especially over the winter when often mice find their way in and have an extremely cosy time amongst the cushions and carpets, along with the spiders. But the waggon is not just a nature reserve and when spring comes the doors are flung open, and the fresh air and sun stream in to disturb them. Out come the dusters, wood polishes, carpet sweeper and window cleaner from the special storage place and everything is given a good spring clean.

My garden room is much more than just an addition to the house and garden because being on wheels it is still used as a travelling home. Every year my mother and I go off to the Netley Marsh steam rally held near Southampton, where all the local steam engines gather for three days. Entertainments include fun fairs, trade stalls, tractors, hot air balloons, and jazz nights, to name but a few, with all the money raised going to local charities. With the aid of a Land-Rover, or occasionally a steam engine, we hit the road and the waggon is back in its element.

I have been a steam enthusiast since I was about seven-years old and as a child at the steam rallies held at home used to enjoy getting black and dirty from the coal. In contrast to the times the waggon is berthed in the garden, the rally meetings we attend are noisy affairs. You hear the shouting of the children, the putt-putt noise of the chugging engines and once we were entertained by full-blast music from a fairground organ parked next door to us.

At the rally, once I have managed to climb on to the roof to put on the chimney, a good fire is lit up using peat blocks or coal, or if the weather is hot, a brazier is lit outside by the steps to heat up the water. Black smuts from the steam engines pour into the waggon blackening both us and the lace curtains, and necessitating the constant use of our beautiful, antique, portable washbasin.

At these steam rallies we meet all the old fairground people who recount stories of times past. Some come and reminisce on how they were brought up in huge families in just such a waggon; some simply come to be curious; but quite a few people remember the waggon as it was when owned by the showman, and we hear how at one time it was pulled by two Suffolk Punches.

Everwhere we go people's curiosity is aroused and prying eyes wide with wonderment are constantly peering over the door. I am convinced that if I should ever find myself without a home to live in, I would have no problem surviving in the old waggon on the highways and by-ways. In my case I would combine waggon and caravan tradition by adorning myself in a gypsy-style outfit and ladening myself down with gold ear-rings and bangles and, of course, with a crystal ball, I could do a roaring trade in fortune telling. I fancy myself reading the tea-leaves, with the pot constantly on the brew, and using only the best, but rather chipped, china.

'Yes, come in dear, sit yourself down and make yourself at home. All original dear, lived here all my life, one of fourteen children. My Dad used to make us sleep under the van, what a life, but you know dear I wouldn't give it up for all the tea in China, how about you?'

Thus my act would continue, and the tea-leaves sincerely read, I would earn my keep, never be lonely, and travel the world.

On reflection, one of the things that might deter me from leaping at such a life would be the lack of a bathroom and missing the hot baths I so love. But fortunately I do have a house and a bathroom to go home to. So the waggon remains a luxurious garden room, gilded and flower filled, situated in a wonderful garden where our quails, bantams and geese wander about. From my garden room window with its pretty chintz curtains I can look over to the meadow beyond where the Jacob sheep graze, and on to the marsh that reaches down to the sea.

Mary Montagu sits on the steps of her garden room waggon at home in the New Forest.

ROBERT KIME

*Robert Kime is an antique dealer and decorator. He is married
to Helen Nicoll, the best-selling author of children's books.
Together with their two children they live in an eighteenth-
century redbrick farmhouse on the edge of the
Marlborough Downs in Wiltshire.*

MY FRIEND, Christopher Gibbs, once owned a charming small watercolour of a conservatory at Farnley Hall in Yorkshire by J.M.W.Turner which he had painted for his friend and patron Walter Fawkes 'to carry about in his pocket book'. This drawing is illustrated on page 128 of John Cornforth's *English Interiors 1790–1848*. It shows tiered rows of potted plants reaching to a roof lit by several Chinese and gothick lanterns hanging at different heights. Unfortunately my pocket book was not adequate for the drawing, but it did serve as the inspiration of our garden room. The combination of the exotically theatrical and the seriously botanical themes blend marvellously in Turner's drawing so that the conservatory turns away from being a greenhouse in which plants are forced to flower, into a pleasure room for sitting and eating in.

Another friend and architect, Mary Lou Arscott, helped us to turn what was a tumbled down eighteenth-century redbrick barn set at right angles to the back of the house into a Farnley Hall type room. We made use of a set of gothick windows that I bought at David Hicks' sale at Britwell. They have stained glass borders and very fine copper glazing bars. Morris Hopkins converted them into tall handsome windows which rise on weighted sashes so that the room is joined with the courtyard garden outside. On fine days this gives a feeling of a cloister, cool and sheltered, but because the roof is tiled there is none of the feeling of an unpleasantly humid greenhouse – more of a largish room thirty foot by twelve with five by twelve foot floor to ceiling windows.

The floor of the garden room is the same level as the garden outside and is made from 'commons', the cheapest brick one can buy, laid face up and in panels to break up the space – they drain to a small earth bed on the inside wall. The colour of the walls was achieved by mixing two colours (grey and pink) of ordinary wall plaster and painting it like a wash onto the render. The result produces a grainy texture to the surface, rather like elastoplast, which complements the pink tones of the raw bricks of the floor: walls and ceilings were then completely netted in training wires to support the now resident climbers of stephanotis, plumbago and passion flower. Water is laid on and comes from a large brass tap that spasmodically drips into a stoop of pink Scottish granite that must have once watered the cab horses of Glasgow. Near the tap is a large cast-iron radiator cover with a marble top which supplies enough heat from the central heating system and serves as a warm stand for tender plants. Our garden room, unlike Mr Fawkes', is definitely a compromise botanically; with windows on only two sides and no overhead light, no plant can stand the rigours of permanent residence except for shade-loving climbers.

The room is often used for meals as it is warm and light all the year round. I love gardening in it on wet days, potting up the house bulbs or giving 'intensive care' to some of the ailing residents, but the most frequent occupation is sitting in a Lloyd-loom chair gazing out of the window, listening to the dripping tap and wondering whether to tie in

*Below the meadow, Mr and Mrs Kime in the converted
porch known in the family as 'the bus shelter'.*

more of the *Clematis armandii* and discourage it from strangling the plumbago. Last year it was the other way round but no doubt the scene will change again soon.

The laying out of the paved areas surrounding the garden room was governed by the fact that a large rectangle had been cut out of the high meadow bank, large enough to turn a horse-drawn haycart to deliver and collect its bales from the barn. The area was cleared and a roughly circular area paved with sarsen stone cobbles and flag-stones which once formed part of the floor of a Burnley cotton mill. The surrounding beds in the quadrant corners were banked up so the plants and shrubs would give the effect of being in a hidden bowl that is both sheltered from the wind that blows off the Wiltshire Downs but over the top of the sunken garden, and warm because the walls and floor of this garden are made of stone, so retaining heat.

At the centre of these radiating flagstones is a medieval octagonal stone well head: reputedly part of the belfry or lantern of Durham Cathedral, but taken down in the nineteenth century as the pierced stone traceries were wearing thin, but still quite suitable as openings for white valerian and foxgloves.

On the back wall under the bank facing the back door of the house is a late Regency wrought-iron summer house. It is known by the children as 'the bus shelter', but was once the porch of a grand house in Calne. This is now its third location and we brought it with us when we moved eight years ago. The top and sides are glazed so it is a completely sheltered sitting spot with a large early nineteenth-century garden seat and, in the sum-mer, a hammock. Happily no one was dozing there last winter when a gale blew over a tree and smashed it to pieces. The canopy of the forty-foot tall tree completely filled the garden with the top branches landing inches short of the garden room. None of the plants was damaged, and the twenty-five foot high six-year-old paulownia tree to the right of the (now restored) bus shelter was also untouched. Its large pale green elephant-ear leaves shade *Allium giganteum* and a large late Byzantine marble plaque of twining vine tendrils. Although part of the wall also tumbled, the archi-tectural fragments were mercifully undamaged.

There is a seventeenth-century stone bust of a Roman emperor and also an early eighteenth-century marble cistern nestling under bushes of old striped roses. Round the rim of the cistern is a Greek inscription, the translation of which is 'Wash off your sins not just your face'.

Before entering a smaller terrace yard to the south side of the garden room is a large lead water cistern dated 1718 which has marvellously moulded crests and armorials, and serves to catch soft water for potted plants like stephanotis and camellias that cannot bear lime water from the tap. The path from the hidden circular garden leads directly in front of the garden room and ends at the back door of the main house. This area has a marble-topped table surrounded by Lloyd-loom type armchairs which came from the Cadena Café in Bristol when it closed down. In this area, too, the feeling of now overgrown formality continues with more pots and tiered stands of flowers and fruits. Some of the pots came from the well-known Compton Pottery near Guildford and are dis-tinguished by their art nouveau decoration and line; their durability is incredible for they never seem to crack even though temperatures fell to twenty degrees below last winter. The Dutch baroque carved bench on the other hand comes out with the sun. This seat would have begun life in an elegant hall in the late seventeenth century but it spent a long time in an outhouse and was used as a chicken roost. Occasionally in summer it still reverts to this function as our hens and ducks squeeze through the iron railings that divide this yard from their small paddock and shamelessly crop the wild strawberries. The other great delight for the fowls to shelter in is an enormous hollow tree trunk of witch elm, eight feet in diameter and over three centuries old. It took two cranes and a low-loader to carry it from a field for my wife's birthday present last October.

The general principle behind all of the inte-gration of house and garden owes a lot to Keith Steadman's garden at Wickwar, in particular his use of planting schemes to reinforce a natural

---

Complementary shapes include a Moroccan glass lantern and an arrangement of nine lattice containers on the tiered wooden plant rack.

architecture. Specimens are not isolated for inspection, but are allowed to seed naturally, in this way paradoxically emphasizing the boundaries they spill across and complementing rather than overwhelming the objects round and over which they climb. Plants reinforce architectural features while at the same time threatening to obliterate

them and so there is a tension between rampant nature and human order. Outside, it is the plants which if anything predominate over stonework, paving, benches, statues, whereas inside it is the other way round – but this is no more than a shift of emphasis. In the end neither must be seen to win, and for me the pleasure of my garden lies in active contemplation of the struggle.

A few paces away from the room is a baroque Dutch hall seat. The hedgehog form residing beneath is a brain coral. Chamomile, rock roses, Alchemilla mollis *and wild strawberries flourish with a standard redcurrant bush.*

View from the sunken garden looking back across the courtyard to the west front of the house. The winter garden room was converted from a barn in 1980 (RIGHT).

LADY NEWBOROUGH

Lady Newborough is married to the seventh Baron Newborough. They farm and live at Rhug, a sandstone country house in North Wales.

RHUG IS the farmhouse, and farming is our life. The 2,400 acres and 4,000 ewes with over 12,000 sheep after lambing keep us busy and prevent us sitting too long in the conservatory. The land rises to over 1,000 feet from the Welsh Dee and the plough gets round most of it. Rhug lies 500 feet above sea level in North Wales. It was built in 1799, replacing a much earlier Rhug (to rhyme with league) and was a small classic Georgian house, until the Victorians added wings to every point of the compass!

The conservatory was built onto the south-east side of the house, and thankfully one's forebears used sandstone to harmonize with the existing stone, rather than the dark drab slate stone used for the western additions, including a three-storied clock tower. The conservatory has two rows of sandstone pillars with arches, which complement the pillars of the portico on the north side of Rhug. Above the ornate corbels on the inside pillars, carved and encircled into the sandstone, are quarters of the coat of arms. The outer pillars have circular terracotta plaques of cherubs busily riding dolphins, eagles and beating an anvil, gardening and harvesting. There are sandstone heads of eagles and lions above them. The inner pillars were grooved to take sliding steel shutters. When pulled down, they closed the arches between the pillars. Heavy Victorian wrought-iron embellishments supported glass of tremendous thickness. This part of the conservatory was built on a plinth, twelve feet proud of the wall of the house. The floor

---

Seen from the lawn in summertime, an exterior view of the house with the recent alterations to the original conservatory.

---

was red Victorian tiles with mosaic patterns. A wide stone staircase branching north and south led to the bedrooms above. Backing onto the conservatory was a billiard room cum ballroom. The billiard table could be lowered by means of an hydraulic lift with a game of billiards in progress, and pumped up again without a ball moving – quite a feat of ingenuity.

Tea was eaten in the conservatory before the last war, carried from the far end of the house, on an oak tray with brass bindings, which was a great weight even before the silver teapot, hot-water jug, sugar bowl, sandwiches, muffins, shortbread and cakes were put on it! An old retired housekeeper can remember carrying that tray, when she was young, the weight engraved on her memory.

A decision had to be made in 1971 whether to pull Rhug down or try and restore it to its original size. We decided on total demolition, then changed to partial demolition, whereupon the Victorian Society objected to the removal of the wrought iron part of the conservatory. They were offered it as a gift, and the subject was closed! All the additional wings were then removed, the sandstone with care as it was needed for restoration purposes. The stone structure of the conservatory we left, as it balanced the essential utility area built by us onto the western side of the house. The kitchen in the Georgian house was in the cellar. Now it is three-quarters of the old dining room facing south, and has the finest cornice in Rhug and a beautiful view. One spends a lot of hours in one's kitchen and a good view helps the work.

Gone are the stone staircase and bedrooms above the conservatory, the wrought-iron work, and shattered plate glass. The tile floor which had lifted and erupted like a volcano from the damp

has been replaced by Manchester paving stones, their colour blending with the sandstone. The joints of the pitch-pine beams were leaded, and the sky is the roof! The massive iron pipes which heated the conservatory have been removed, some of the wrought-iron grilles covering the pipes remain, elsewhere the channels have been filled with soil and climbing shrubs and flowers grow when the rabbits allow! The camellias were killed in the bitter winter of 1981/82, in the summer months we have them growing in pots in the conservatory, also oleanders from the West Indies.

Rhug is not the oldest of the Wynn family houses. Bodfean in Caernarfonshire claims that fame, and Bodfean has gone, in the 1960s, as has Glynllifon, the Palladian mansion also in Caernarfonshire which had three full-sized organs in it, and the Botticelli in the butler's pantry – sold for £80 in 1932 when Glynllifon was sold by the Wynns. That Botticelli was brought from Italy to North Wales by the first Lord Newborough and sold by Christies in 1982 for three-quarters of a million. He also built Belan Fort overlooking the narrowest part of the Menai Straits, and garrisoned it with his own army to defend Caernarfon against the French. In memory of those other homes we have incorporated part of them into our Rhug. The porch in the conservatory keeps the study draught free, and logs are stored there. The arched window in the porch came from the stable yard at Glynllifon. In the study the slate mantelpiece is a copy of the one at Ty Cerrig, the farmhouse we lived in whilst Rhug was being restored. The cannon and cannon balls are from Belan Fort. Neither they, nor the much bigger ones on the battery at the Fort were ever used in anger, though the present Lord Newborough was taken to court for firing a cannon ball through the sail of a yacht! Outside the conservatory is an unusual sundial from Bodfean Hall. At Glynllifon and Bodfean there were follys, so Rhug has one. In a small redbrick round house, which was a double-sided loo, sit Mr and Mrs Jones. If unwary guests visit them, they get a trifle wet, as they are fountains, although that is a

Close-up detail of an arch including the capital and plaque, demonstrates the fine restraint achieved in the restoration.

grand description of their aquatic performances.

From the conservatory we can see groups of hardwoods and individual oaks laid out by Humphry Repton. Sadly, the elms have died, their leaves turned yellow in high summer, then died back with Dutch elm disease. When winter comes the pheasants fly off the top of the steep hardwoods at great height and speed, defeating even the best of guns, and live to fly and breed again.

The trout are rising on the lake opposite the conservatory on this warm summer evening, and a mallard duck swims with her fluffy brood behind her. If disturbed, she will pretend she has a broken wing, to distract you from her young. On the island a mute swan sat on seven eggs, the cob hissing and flapping his wings if any one dared get too close to the nest. So many mute swans die of lead poisoning we feed ours daily, helping the cygnets to live, especially as the lake is still short of natural food since dredging it in 1976 with puffing steam engines on either side of the lake. Now in July there are still five well-grown cygnets, no longer fluffy and white, but grey and gawky, until they get their adult plumage. From the lake our eyes travel up to the Berwyn Mountains on the skyline, to where there stands the remains of Liberty Hall, an old lodge built by a Wynn of yore for shooting days. The heather is just turning colour, and the twelfth of August is nearly here again: that wonderful call of the grouse 'go back, go back, go back', the whirr of their wings, the bees in the heather, bilberries, the smell of peat, flies and biting midges. Why has no weaver woven the beautiful brown colour formation of the breast feathers of a grouse into tweed?

About the lake grow bullrushes, forget-me-not, honeysuckle, foxgloves, harebells, meadowsweet, wonderfully named hog-weed, cranes-bill, weasel-snout, and rose-bay willow-herb, which covered every bomb site with pink flowers in cities and towns ransacked by bombing in the last war. The heady scent from lime trees mingles with rose and lily from the more formal garden, and plump peas, broad beans, raspberries and cherry red radishes need picking and pulling in the vegetable garden.

Down on the Dee a fisherman casts his fly hoping for a salmon, a dipper bobs on a stone and a kingfisher flashes by, brilliant cobalt blue and chestnut. A pair of oyster-catchers, newcomers

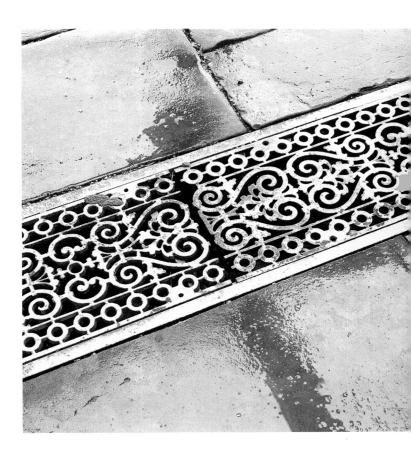

Wrought-iron grilles once covered massive heating pipes and the tiled floor is now replaced with Manchester paving stones.

this year, quiver in flight, red-billed, smart in black and white – and oft repeat their shrill call 'kewick, kewick, kwirr'. But where are the dragonflies of one's youth, and all those wonderful coloured butterflies: red admirals, peacocks, silver-washed fritillaries, painted ladies, brimstones and clouded yellows? And the moths: cinnebar, green forester, tiger, red underwing and frightening death's-head hawk-moth, where are they? But the bats still flit by at dusk, coming out as the swifts are lost to view as the sun sinks behind the mountains.

The stable clock strikes half past three
Gone are the staff that brought us tea!!!

From the arches of the loggia to the green park land, lake and blue hills beyond (OVERLEAF).

CHARMIAN STIRLING

*Charmian Stirling is the daughter of Lord and Lady George Scott
and is an artist who specializes in portraits of children.
She lives in an early Victorian house in Lambeth.*

BOUGAINVILLEA, stephanotis, jasmine and plumbago, all common flowers of warmer climates than ours, are beginning to flourish abundantly on their trellises, tumbling from the ceiling and intertwining recklessly; while on the floor orange trees, lilies and masses of scented geraniums live in big tubs that can be moved out into the garden in the summer.

None of the plants in my conservatory is rare but I love all those that can make it a fantasy place for me. It is delicious to sit among them and let the scent of orange blossom and jasmine waft you away from the bleakest winter day in London to the holiday world of perpetual sunshine and flowers. I find it particularly good for morale from November to March to heat up the conservatory to a tropical temperature and enjoy going rapidly bankrupt amongst bowls of early bulbs – the heavier-scented the better – such as hyacinths and paper-white narcissus. It all helps one to forget the depressing fact that London is on the same latitude as Labrador in the Northern Hemisphere and the Falkland Islands in the South. Some people call their conservatories winter gardens, which is a far prettier and more apt name for some, but my conservatory functions very much all the year round and I use it as much in the summer as the winter.

In keeping with the holiday nostalgia, I have found it to be a wonderful place for my beloved collection of shells. I do not think that Mary Mary was quite contrary at all and was absolutely right

Double doors link dining room with studio; the pelmet materials and wallpaper come from Osborne & Little, the floor tiles are Portuguese.

about shells and flowers mixing well in a garden; and they look particularly pretty amongst the ferns and trailing greenery of a conservatory. Also they must feel so happy being watered all the time. I have gathered shells from every beach I have ever been to, from my favourite (cowries galore) in the north-west of Scotland to the Tahitian coral islands (more cowries but slightly bigger). I must admit that one or two I have found on the beaches of Peter Jones.

There are other things in the conservatory like an easel, boxes of paints and pencils, piles of paper and sketch books, and an enormous draughtsman's chest that is meant to contain them but that does not quite manage to as they seem to overflow onto most available surfaces. The reason why I have these unlikely objects around is that my conservatory is also a studio and it is all the fault of the local planning permission people that I have one at all. They would not let us build a studio in the garden behind our house and, as I seriously needed somewhere to paint, their stern refusal was a great disappointment. We were then intrigued and excited to learn that we would be allowed to build a conservatory instead.

I was a bit doubtful at first whether it would work as a studio for, although it is wonderful to have unlimited light for painting, you do require it to come from one direction only; and, particularly for drawing portraits, which is what I do most of, you do need the white and unchanging north light. My other worry was that, if I had a conservatory, I would want to grow plants and the damp atmosphere necessary to keep them happy and healthy would not be any good at all for my conté crayons and Ingres paper. It was for this reason that we devised a double conservatory with one part to be

used entirely as a studio, curtained and screened against unwanted sunbeams; with doors to an annex where there could be wooden staging for putting seed trays, and as many plants as could be squeezed in, and where I could squirt the hose around happily without destroying my drawings.

The firm who made the conservatory first constructed the framework in their workshop and brought it here in huge sections. They then had to haul these over two garden walls and stagger with them through our kind neighbours' gardens, the pieces being too big to get through our house. The foundations and floor had been laid by builders who were working here at the time and the whole framework was put together in two days.

We now had an oblong glass studio facing north and south with a three-sided annex to the east built right into the garden, the lawn being almost flush with the staging, the two parts with a glass partition and double doors between them. The big problem of how to shut out the light from the south and east I think we have solved by more or less turning the studio into a tent. I used thick white ticking for the roof curtains which hang from brass rings sliding along brass poles. There is a double thickness on the south side so when those curtains are shut and the north left open, it gives a pretty good light for drawing. The curtains round the sides are of Laura Ashley pink and white ticking and there is a sort of festoon curtain in the angle of the roof that can be let down.

Unless I am drawing a portrait, all the side curtains are tied back or up, whereas the roof curtains are nearly always shut. People do not realize how boilingly hot a conservatory can become with just a little sunshine, and these tented curtains give a prettily diffused light, protecting plants and people from too much heat and dazzle in summer, while helping enormously to keep the heat in in the winter. We have ordinary radiators run on the house central heating system with a separate thermostat. It has to be quite hot for my sitters, who are often children and it really has to be warmer for them than for most delicate

Victorian-style cresting and finial on the conservatory which projects into the south-facing garden. The pink rose in the foreground is Zéphirine Drouhin.

plants. At one time I had painted the garden wall of the patio facing the conservatory white, thinking it would reflect even more light back into the studio, but I found that when the sun shone it was too dazzling for my sitters to look at without screwing their eyes up into tiny slits and so it is now painted a soft pinkish colour.

There are double doors from the dining room to the conservatory and then more double doors leading out into the garden. They open onto a small and, on three sides, extremely sheltered patio, from which steps lead up to the main part of the garden. This patio is in the summer really an extension of the conservatory, as the doors stand open most of the time and my precious pots and tubs of regale lilies and orange trees cluster round them. Here I have planted more tokens of Mediterranean nostalgia with a vine, fig tree, olive tree, more jasmine, a lemon verbena, rosemary bushes and other herbs, *Clematis montana*, honeysuckle and the rose Zéphirine Drouhin. There is a wisteria which has grow all along the trellis on the garden wall and is about to start climbing up the house. Ivy-leaved geraniums, fuchsias, tobacco plants, pinks and pansies are also dug into every available pot, and morning glories climb the climbers. This is the only place in the garden where there is a lot of colour. The main part is mostly very green, which I love to have in London. The flowers are pale luminous pinks, creams, off-white and green and, as long as the lawn is mown, I like the whole thing to be a bit jungly.

I had no idea how much I would enjoy having a conservatory. Certainly my interest in greenhouses did not start very early, although living in Wiltshire as a child, there was an orangery slightly away from the house which my mother adored. We children were utterly uninterested in it unless our mother had found one of her favourite hedgehogs, which often seemed to wander in and would then be cossetted with saucers of bread and milk. Apart from that we were much more fascinated by the potting shed and its dark mysteries. We used to engage the gardener there in endless conversations while he was potting out seedlings or eating his lunch, which he brought tied up in a red spotted handkerchief.

The first time I was enchanted by the glamour of a conservatory or winter garden, as he called it, was visiting Cecil Beaton's at Reddish House, also in Wiltshire, which was so pretty and full of ferns, palms and cascades of jasmine. I had always thought of a greenhouse as somewhere where flowers were grown to plant out in the garden or bring into the house, and the idea of sitting amongst all these luxurious fronds seemed both sophisticated and romantic.

Back to my own house of glass, which is rather austere as conservatories go. I would love it to encompass a tropical forest of palms and vines, but this is a working studio so I cannot have the strange greenish light that too much overhead growth would produce, nor risk any drips from hanging baskets or creepers. The plan to keep the two parts entirely separate does not really work.

Corner of the studio shows an ornately carved wooden seat from India which was found in a Doune antique shop and has been painted white.

More and more plants congregate in the studio as the results of my over-enthusiastic planting are squeezed out of their appointed area and into my working space. It becomes so crowded in winter that my sitters and I can be found embowered like Douanier Rousseau tigers among the tender plants and shrubs that have been brought inside to escape the frosts. The fuller it is of plants, the more I enjoy it, and find it an endless source of excitement, as all the watering cans, flowerpots, baskets, trowels and shells are interesting to paint, as are the china bowl and ewer sets given me by my mother-in-law. The jugs are ideal for watering, while the huge bowls hold a large amount of bulbs in the spring and in summer some are planted with white campanula while others are piled with pot pourri.

I have various favourite pieces of furniture in the conservatory, such as a carved wood Indian seat bought in a junk shop in Scotland years ago, painted white and extremely fragile and a big Chippendale armchair, in which my sitters pose and which also doubles as a dining-room chair. There is a hat stand hung about with ancient straw relics of Ascot, weddings and Italian holidays, and a dog basket which is very important as my whippet gets upset if she cannot sit beside me while I am working and, as she would not dream of lying on the floor, if the basket is in another room, she comes to stare reproachfully at me, interrupting the sitting until I go and fetch it for her.

There are many things that I would still like to do in here. One is to get a few comfortable basket-like chairs so that other people can enjoy the place as much as I do as, at the moment, I have it all rather selfishly to myself. Occasionally it is used as an overflow dining room when I have a rare big dinner party and this entails a lot of moving around of furniture but it is worth it as conservatories make pretty dining rooms. I imagine it will gradually evolve with time and new ideas, and I can only say that, in the three years since the garden room was built, it is hard for me to decide whether the planting side or the painting side has given me more pleasure.

A view of the inside of the conservatory showing the tented curtains across the glass roof.

MYLES THOROTON HILDYARD

*Myles Thoroton Hildyard qualified as a barrister but became a farmer
after the war. He is unmarried. Flintham Hall near Newark in
Nottinghamshire has been the family home since the
eighteenth century. It is an early medieval house first rebuilt in
Jacobean times, later doubled in size to become a Georgian mansion
and in 1852 it was faced with stone outside and decorated inside.*

LEWIS WYATT began designing various alterations and new buildings including a conservatory for my great-great-grandfather in
1825 and work started on the library cellars in
1829. Within a year my ancestor died, owing a
quarter of a million. The conservatory was never
built. It was to have lain at an angle to the house,
joined to it by a colonnade, which would have
masked the east side of the old house. For a
generation this end of the house must have looked
unfinished since the south and east wings did not
join up properly. In 1853 my great-grandfather
began spending the money his father hadn't left
him. He faced the outside of the house in stone,
spending enough to build a new house with one
hundred and thirty five rooms. Inside he reduced
the number of water closets from seven to two and
he took out the bedrooms over the library to make
a room which in his day must have been unheat-
able. Now it just takes enough kilowatts to power
a row of houses and a tree or two in the grate.

My great-grandfather built the present conservatory next to the library, pulling down part of
the east wing. It is easy to see that the architect
T.C.Hine was influenced by the recently built
Crystal Palace. It juts out to the south. Half can be
seen through glazed arches or from an Italianate
gallery from the library and in this half is a large
white marble fountain. The overflow of this is now

blocked and we get floods when the fountain is
allowed to play too fast – the water ends up in the
boiler-room below and has to be baled out by
hand. The western and southern sides of the
projection, which are visible from the garden, are
built in stone and glass, the east side is brick
outside. The roof is semi-circular, formed of curved
sheets of glass resting on cast-iron ribs. The
conservatory is forty-seven by twenty-two feet
and forty feet high. It was designed to take palms
and there still were two in my youth. They were
not pretty from underneath and threatened the
roof, so my father had them out. They are still
lying down the garden fifty years later, apparently
quite sound. Apart from the fountain, there is a
central bed where the palms grew and narrow beds
on the east side under large arched windows and
sheets of mirror glass which reflect, and must once
have reflected much more brilliantly, the two
libraries and their chandeliers. In these beds grow
climbers thirty-feet high, a blue and white plumbago, three bignonias and cobaea. The blue plumbago and one bignonia are probably original. My
father paved the central bed with tiles brought
from the ruined house on the island in the lake.
This left the conservatory very bare and we never
sat there as the roof leaked. Along one wall were
iron stands for rows of pot plants. I removed these
as they are a bore to water and the place is pretty
full without them. I replanted the central bed with
daturas, abutilons, tree ferns and a mimosa which
is now in its turn threatening the roof. I also
covered the north wall with creepers, jasmine and

*An exterior view, which shows the full magnificence and
perfect symmetry of the building.*

so on, growing from a trough as there is no bed.

Round the fountain I have ginger plants in pots. There are camellias in white-painted orange boxes on either side of the door onto the terrace. I expect the boxes came from the orangery down the garden, which is now roofless, and we have more camellias and *rhododendron* 'fragrantissimum' in pots about the place. They are apt to get taken into the house, which practically kills them. I paved part of the central bed and there is room for eight to eat there. It is very pretty at night when the surrounding jungle is floodlit. Hanging from the roof are nine large baskets of flowers. The conservatory was originally lit by gas. The gas jets are the stamens of porcelain arum lilies with bronze leaves each side of a porcelain lady called Dorothea. They were in the Crystal Palace. Because my conservatory is part of the house it had to be maintained, unlike some famous conservatories which are now mostly all gone, I believe. Some time in the nineteenth century, although my family were very short of money, the roof was remodelled, the number of ribs was doubled and the size of each pane halved.

There isn't much room for furniture in the conservatory. There is a heavily carved, probably teak, settee painted white, which no-one sits on. For dinner parties we bring in everything. As a matter of fact I have a range of vineries down the garden which I think are prettier. I don't sit there either but I am thinking of putting in a swimming pool. I generally bathe in the lake when the weather is warm enough but the trouble is chlorine kills plants and I envisage swimming in the pool under a cloud of sweet peas and morning glory.

The vineries are heated in part by Calor Gas but the conservatory is still heated by its original hot water pipes under the floor gratings, run off an oil-fired boiler. I am told they are as good as anything. It is thermostatically controlled and, unlike the house, has to run all night in cold weather, which is expensive. I only aim to keep it above freezing. Because of the great height and amount of glass this is difficult enough and I wish I could put in some sort of ceiling for the winter. The con-

Glimpse of arches, columns and climbing plants within the conservatory.

servatory is ventilated in hot weather by an electric fan under the roof. It can get very hot. I would like to grow bananas and climbers such as bougainvillea and thunbergia if it were hotter in winter. It was not heated at all during the war years. I wore a Russian bear-skin ankle length coat when I came on leave.

I restored the roof of the conservatory a few years ago and this time the panes were set in rubber gaskets and more or less stopped leaking. (I got a grant towards this from the Historic Buildings Council.) The panes are curved and had to be made to order. The manufacturer delivered frosted glass which I rejected, which wasted time. I had the panes made in quarter-inch plate glass. The thin glass my father had used for replacements was always breaking. I tried first using plastics, which after a time turned milky white in the sun and looked terrible. Birds used to find a way in and build nests in the creepers, making a great din and mess.

The work took months longer than promised. I had to make polythene tents and heat them with Calor Gas and while I was abroad a heavy fall of snow broke the mimosa tree. We treated the glass inside to prevent algae growing on it. This is a bore on the glass of the walls, as they are so high to reach. So also is pruning. The cobaea is particularly tiresome, as it sends shoots round roof girders and basket wires which, if allowed to remain, become in a year or two too thick to remove easily.

My great-uncle had three or four gardeners, several semi-incapacitated, and, although the flower garden was nothing much and after the first war the lawns were unmown, the glass houses and kitchen gardens were kept up and pot plants grown for the conservatory. Everything that could be sold was sold and I do not remember our eating the peaches or grapes. I never met my great-uncle, though I was thirteen when he died. However, my father, who lived in London, was often here. It is one of my regrets that he never asked him what the house was like before 1853.

My mother dreaded accompanying him, the old horse and brougham plodding out from Newark railway station, the dark house full of stuffed birds, surrounded by wellingtonias, hip baths, and my great-uncle, who was very low church and religious, speaking very, very slowly.

The daylight from the conservatory lends a beautiful, rather mysterious illumination to the library (ABOVE).

We came here in 1928. My father saw no future for the place but wanted his children brought up here. We galloped every day along the Trent Hills, every drawer was full of treasures, old rusty swords, old rolled-up pedigrees. My mother soon abolished the stuffed birds and I made a museum for them and other junk upstairs on the unused top floor. She replaced linoleum with carpets, turfed the naked plaster Venus out of the hall (how can my great-uncle have allowed that? But it was very dark), made a pretty drawing room, put eighteenth-century furniture in the dining room (the Victorian furniture is back again now) and generally worked like a Trojan, inside and out. Indeed my parents were both great workers, my father, a judge, beavering away at trusts for which no one ever thanked him, improving the farm which never paid, taking over the park and home

Plants whether potted, hanging or climbing all combine with a pedestal to make an interesting balance of form and shades.

farm which had been let, and, together with my
mother, laying crazy paving and building dry
stone walls. My mother was very keen on gardening and made a large border and rose garden. My
father made three tennis courts. I have undone
much of their work but I admire them deeply.

I would not say I was a happy child – we do not
know if Adam and Eve were happy in Paradise.
My mother dragged us, my brother and me, to
parties, but we had no friends. I do not suppose we
were in the least friendly. We knew we were poor, a
dreadful strain, living in a hideous house. Out of
the corner of his eyes, my brother had glimpses of
another, outside, world. He ended up as an ambassador. I remained totally immersed in my little
world of dogs and making paths in woods.

What of school, university, the war? Well, I
came back here, each time. I took over the farm,
my father died, I expanded the farm, putting back
into it anything I made, it was a success (so far). I
made the house easier to run, re-arranged and
redecorated it as I could, altered and extended the
gardens, planted trees, buried dogs, travelled. It is
the life I wanted.

Plants line the route to a quiet place to sit.

PAMELA BULLMORE

*Pamela Bullmore is a garden designer who lives and works in
London. She is married to Jeremy Bullmore, the chairman of
the J. Walter Thompson (UK) advertising company.
Their weekend house is a seventeenth-century stone farmhouse
on the banks of the River Nadder in Wiltshire.*

M Y CONSERVATORY is very young – only
two years old. It is small, eleven by fourteen foot, and is what the manufacturers
choose to call 'a standard module'. Not exactly
a romantic description for my silver wedding
present and Life's Dream.

During the week we live in a flat and work in
London – my husband in advertising and myself as
a garden designer – so ours has to be a weekend
conservatory. It is certainly not ideal to grow
plants under glass with minimum care five days a
week, but it presented an interesting challenge and
seemed well worth trying.

Late spring and early summer with their capri-
cious temperatures are the most hair-raising
times. A few warm days in midweek can make life
for the plants almost intolerable. Watering is of
course the gravest problem, but I am exceptionally fortunate to have a kind, caring, dependable
friend who lives nearby and, when it's hot, goes in
every day. I do not think that the automatic
watering for pots has been very satisfactory, but
now there is a really good German system, which I
am installing this year.

The conservatory is built against the east side of
the house, half of it bulging a bit beyond the house,
so that it gets the evening sun. It leads off the
sitting room through a glazed door, and at the west
angle of its bulge there are double doors opening
onto wide shallow steps down to the paved terrace
in front of the house. These doors open outwards
and fold right back, so that in summer the garden
and conservatory are in close communion. Unfortunately, building regulations allowed us only two
small borders against the north wall, and the rest

of the 'ground' is paved in stone, which means that
most of the plants have to be grown in pots of
varying sizes. There are points for lamps should we
need them, but somehow, when you've watched
the sun set, the dusk gather, and then the evening
sky, man-made light seems all wrong. You can talk
and have a drink very well in darkness. In summer
the moths come out of hiding and secretly rustle
among the plants and bats weave swirling patterns
in the sky above. However, this is not to
everyone's taste. Some friends can't bear moths
near them and loathe bats at any distance, so we
have to retire to the safety and bright lights of the
sitting room.

At the north end of the conservatory there is an
old stone wall that used to support a rickety,
corrugated iron-roofed shed for the old farm cider
press. We moved the cider press and made a door
in the wall, which now connects the conservatory
to what is called 'the potting shed', but, strictly
speaking, is an unheated lean-to glazed room with
a potting bench.

When planning the conservatory the most important thing was to organize it so that conditions
were as conducive as possible to growing plants
that would not necessarily receive daily attention.
A tap, a small hose on a reel, damp-proof electrical
points, thermostatically-controlled vents, blinds
for shading the roof and fans were essential. I also
wanted a thermostatically-controlled heater that
prevented the temperature dropping below 45° F.

*Time to give the plants a drink and a flotilla of watering-
cans foregather.*

Then came the choosing of plants that would be able to exist for five days of the week with minimum attention. I wanted attractive foliage plants and flowers with scent throughout the year.

I wanted a tree to give a strong permanent feature. Lovely as climbers are, they lack the robust splendour of a tree. I chose a mimosa, *Acacia baileyana*, which is an easy, untempera-

January yellow mimosa around the door leading from conservatory to potting shed.

mental tree. It is planted in a corner where there is a proper bed for it to grow in, and by a happy chance it can be seen through the sitting-room door. At Christmas time the first faintly scented yellow fluffy flowers appear, but the best thing about this variety is its exquisite frilly foliage which hardly needs the embellishment of flowers. It changes colour from green to turquoise to silver according to the light. By moonlight it looks as if it is made of grey feathers. I also needed two evergreen climbers to grow in the bed at the foot of the potting shed wall. I decided on a jasmine, *Jasminum polyanthum*, which flowers in February and March and is wickedly scented. The scent is so powerful that it escapes into the house. The other choice is *Lapageria rosea*, which flowers in summer and autumn. The flowers are elegantly slim bells, about three inches long and bright raspberry pink; no smell, but once seen never forgotten. Grown in a pot, *Tetrastigma voinerianum* climbs with amazing vigour along one of the roof supports.

I am thrilled to discover just how soon spring comes in a conservatory garden. In January, the chairs are moved into the house until the end of February and tiered, circular, green metal staging is moved in as a centre piece. It is my fantasy to cover it with pots of early flowers and have a roundabout of colour in January and February. Not easy, but never mind, it is a good challenge. March and April are particularly good months; it may be raw and blustery outside, but bursts of crude bright sunshine quickly warm up the indoor garden. By the end of May, many of the plants go outside on the steps to enjoy real sun and rain, leaving more space for us.

Watering cans are pleasing practical objects and last year, when working in Provence, I was extremely pleased to find a large fat oval French can to add to my collection. It has an enormous rose that gushes out a miniature tropical rain storm. I love the smell and the dark rings of dampness on the stone floor after watering. The cans are always left full, some with rain-water for particularly fussy plants, and stand around the floor among the pots in a nonchalant manner. They are very nice to look at, and when it is hot their evaporation helps the humidity in the conservatory. Also helping with the humidity is a very modest pool and so much evaporation takes place

On a wet winter's day, through a glass happily to the contents of the conservatory.

in summer that it needs to be topped up every weekend.

The pool is the original old stone sink that was in the kitchen when we bought the house eighteen years ago; since then it had been outside in the garden, planted with sedums. When I was planning the conservatory it caught my eye and I realized its possibilities as a pool. One side of it is very worn, giving the edge a slight curve. It was moved in and supported on a large stone in a concreted reservoir in the floor.

I am always on the look out for attractive ornaments for other people's gardens and I remembered that I had seen a charming old lead pump water box and spout in Hammersmith some months before. By an amazing chance it was still there. I could hardly believe my luck. It was fixed behind the sink pool. A small pump in the reservoir underneath pumps the water up into the water box, to pour gently out of the spout into the pool, which then overflows. The overflowing water glides over the smooth worn edge and trickles back into the reservoir. You can hear the trickling water in the sitting room. We are used to it and like the sound, but sometimes visitors find it quite irritating, like the sound of a dripping tap, which is not quite what I planned.

I have always been entranced by conservatories. They have a charming still-life quality which is peaceful and escapist. To me they mean plants; pampered, privileged plants in a decorative, intimate, indoor garden; to please the eye and to relax in. As a child I loathed staying in London. It meant shopping at Daniel Neal or Gorringes for school uniform and catching the school train from Victoria. The only good thing about London was visiting Kew Gardens. I adored the Glass Houses: they were paradise. Some of my childhood was very happily spent in Burma. My father had a wonderful collection of orchids; he collected them from the wild and grew them, cleverly bound into the forks and branches of trees. Cymbidiums grew in pots, alternately with ferns, on the verandahs round the house. Now I have these orchids growing in my conservatory. They flower in January

Dark green modern metal staging by Conran forms a three-tier support to potted plants.

and February with the hyacinths, narcissi, primulas, cyclamen and miniature iris. Actually it is rather a pity that they flower at the same time because they do look a bit strange and exotic with the familiar spring flowers, so I keep them as far apart as possible. My conservatory is really too full of plants for its size. As a designer I should know better and no doubt I shall mend my ways in time.

There are many unexpected delights I have discovered about having an indoor garden. Its additional environment is especially enjoyable in winter: when you go from the warm domesticity of the house into the cool, still, greenness and sweet smell of the indoor garden, and then out into the real garden with its cold sharp air and the wind, with birds and the special damp smell of hedges and trees. I find it curiously pleasing to have two completely different gardens, separated only by panes of glass. Pots of plants that have been outside for the summer return with self-sown seeds that sometimes sprout into parsley, pansies and chickweed. Undesirable weeds are removed, but chickweed takes on a different status under glass with good food and drink. It grows huge and luscious, is a delicate bright green and tumbles over the sides of pots in the most decorative way and stays fresh all winter. Early butterflies and bees come in to enjoy the windless warmth and the flowers. The hum of bees is very soporific. There is, however, one unexpectedly unpleasant discovery. Conservatories get very messy with dead leaves, fallen petals, dead woodlice and cobwebs in the corners of the window frames and the difficult-to-reach roof panes. They have to be kept clean and tidy and it has to be done every weekend in summer, a routine just as awful as housework.

Another thing I have learned is that when people hear you have a conservatory so often the first thing they say is: 'How lovely. Do you have wonderful lunch parties in it?' The idea appals me. Regrettably I am far too unrelaxed for that kind of thing. Supposing a guest pushed back a chair, I would agonize, and knocked the bud off the *Datura suaveolens*? I hastily explain that ours is too small for entertaining. They lose interest immediately. To my mind a conservatory is the place for a good read, a game of backgammon, conversation, a doze or a think. Tea is all right, and a drink at the end of the day is excellent, but nothing more ambitious.

VISCOUNTESS HAMBLEDEN

*Lady Hambleden is the only daughter of Ambassador and
Contessa Attolico di Adelfia. She is married to Viscount Hambleden,
head of the W. H. Smith family. They live in the Manor House at
Hambleden, an early seventeenth-century flint and brick house
extended during Regency and Victorian times and again in the 1960s.*

FOR TWO MONTHS of the year we have a scented house from the jasmine in the conservatory. First there is the flowering, then afterwards, even when the petals have dried, the scent lingers so strongly that if the conservatory doors are open you can smell the scent from the front door at the opposite end of the house.

The smell of jasmine takes me back to Italy. When I grew up we had a lovely house in Rome near the Appian Way as well as one in the country. In Rome there were french windows onto a terrace where I remember once having lunch on Christmas Day under the pergola. The place was full of the fragrance of Mediterranean flowers and jasmine grew close to the house. The rooms seemed full of light. I never thought that in England it would be possible to have a room which captured the Italian feeling so well unless one built one, and now that we have, it has gradually become a part of our life.

The atmosphere of the conservatory here is both English and Italian. It is sophisticated and exotic, rather in the way orangeries must have felt when they were first built here by the English and in this cold climate people could be entertained in a most unusual setting with strange new flowers and trees. In summer the glass doors are open onto the terrace and the lawn and a graceful link is formed between house and garden.

The conservatory was built in the 1960s and so we were quite pioneers as the revival had not yet come about. It was my husband's idea in conjunc-

*Lady Hambleden below the white jasmine festooned glass
dome in the conservatory.*

tion with Martyn Beckett who is a great friend and used to come here to shoot. Harry is a man of great taste, he wanted to build something for himself and Martyn seemed the ideal man to create it. The idea came around after a nice shooting weekend when everybody was feeling very happy, full of ideas and imagination. It was not at all difficult to decide where to put the room because we had a terraced space behind the library which we did not know what to do with, so we were able to keep the retaining wall and make a proper end to the house. The process took a year and the proportions when finished were perfect.

When Harry decided to build the conservatory all the children were very young and I thought it would be nice to have a playroom as well, so we made this addition on higher ground directly behind the conservatory with its own separate entrance and a hallway and steps to follow down to link the two places. The windows of the playroom are in a gothick style to match the Victorian part of the house. About five years ago, after the children had all grown up, we decided to transform their room into a billiard room. When we first discussed the whole scheme of our building over twenty years ago there was an idea of reaching the conservatory through a big door to be put into the library. I was against this as it had just been decorated and with the dark green walls it makes a comfortable room for winter. Also the addition of a door would have meant no space for the big sofa which is set against the far wall, so in the end, very reluctantly, we decided to have the new place reached by a separate passage, or directly from the garden. Because the gardeners can enter the

conservatory from outside it makes looking after the place easier and there is no worry about dirtying the carpets indoors. The floor is made of a pinkish Lancashire stone and can be easily washed down.

We have had several parties in the conservatory and it is a place where we can easily seat sixty or seventy people. When we are a large number I arrange for a whole series of small tables seating eight to replace the main circular table. It needs quite a lot of organization to arrange meals in there: with the setting of the tables, the steps down from the passage and the transport of food either down the long passage from the kitchen or, in summer, through the garden.

Detail of the striped pelmet and curtains designed by the late John Fowler, and wood trellis, their faded colours gently blending with surrounding plants.

Where hallway meets conservatory, a wallpaper with matching border by Colefax & Fowler.

Waiting for the party to begin, a row of empty seats including a Goan dining chair and rattan armchair.

On a fine, crisp day in winter, a view to show the conservatory as adjunct to the rear of the house (RIGHT).

One of the most magic evenings we ever had was in February of the year of the electricity strikes. I went to all the churches around here and borrowed candlesticks, then we lit up the house by candles and sixty people came to spend the evening by flickering light, surrounded by warmth and flowers with a blizzard swirling round outside the glass.

We had lunch for the Italian president two years ago. I knew in advance he would be here for only one and a half hours, so this was a case where the timing of the food relied on dishes that could be quickly and easily served. For that occasion we had an Italian flan and a water ice. Then we always have lunch for the shoot in the conservatory and we have had several parties for the boys and barbecues in the summer and we gave a supper party in there on the night before my eldest son's wedding. For my mother-in-law's eightieth birthday party, when the Queen Mother came, I

arranged the seating plan of the tables by the names of flowers rather than numbers. It was an attractive idea but it did not quite work since there were inevitably a few friends who had not the faintest idea what, say, a freesia looked like and only found their seat after much searching.

Sometimes after dark we draw the striped curtains in the conservatory to create a completely different mood. Covering the windows in there was something I would never have thought of, but it was John Fowler who insisted and he was right because the addition of curtains, striped with the same blue-grey as the walls and the trellis, makes the place into a complete room. The colours have all faded pleasingly to make a peaceful background. At the time I questioned the strength of the bright colours John put on the walls both in there and in other rooms, for instance the pink of the drawing room and my Chinese yellow sitting room, but he would tell me to leave everything as he had done it because it would fade correctly. He knew how to mix paints and the results show so many years later. I worked with John on the redecoration of the house for two years first in the 1950s, soon after we were married, when I was very young and would have had no idea how to tackle such a responsibility myself. He gave me great confidence and was fond of saying he would get the bones right but it was up to us to clutter rooms with living. Later, after the conservatory was built, it was he who worked out the correct proportions of the round table within the round room and then it was made up for us by our carpenter.

The objects in the room, like the plants, are really a happy mish-mash and were put together in the years soon after the place was built. There are Venetian lanterns, a *cloisonné* peacock plate on the wall, a large refectory table and a mixture of garden furniture including some Goan chairs. One of my best sources for finding things was Geoffrey Bennison and I first met him when he had a stall in Islington market. We became close friends and because of his particular style I would call him the complete Renaissance man. Then more places I used to hunt were at the Portmeirion Shop and Jack Reffold's in Pont Street, two antique shops which no longer exist, and at Jack Wilson in Chelsea.

To begin with we had to coax the plants to flower. The climbers would creep up the wall but they would rarely bloom and this was particularly the case with the jasmine. The gardener, who has since retired but remains in charge of the conservatory routine, had the good suggestion of training the plants into the direct light beneath the glass dome. His solution was to build a wrought-iron circle and suspend it from the outer rim of the dome by a series of iron brackets. Our local ironmonger made the circle, since when the plants have been trained onto it and they flourish. In summer months we add to the display with hanging baskets of busy lizzies.

There is no special irrigation system and the watering must all be done laboriously by hand, with extra ladders in summer to reach the baskets. There is controlled ventilation, and also a humidifier which prevents the insects and plant diseases, but what is very important is the special heating system which has been laid in the troughs underneath the iron floor grilles. In winter the room is normally heated to exactly the same temperature as the house but in extreme cold we turn on the booster heating system which has been installed around the central glass dome.

Although I use other rooms for reading, writing and so on, it is nice to feel the conservatory is there full of plants and to know it is an integral part of this old house we have added ourselves. People say a conservatory is less work because it is an unlikely place to find weeds, but we find there is always more to do in there. We specialize in roses at Hambleden and all year round there is work to be done in the garden outside. Indoors the roots of our original planting are beginning to turn back on themselves which is a new problem to tackle and if the climbers are left untended the place turns into a jungle. The work in the conservatory, like the garden, is never done and for me that is one of its greatest delights. On reflection the room exceeds my first dreams because it has been such an obvious success.

On the rim of a jardinière *with gilded wood rams' heads, shafts of midwinter sun pierce the stillness of the indoor garden.*

SUSAN GERNAEY

Susan Gernaey is a freelance garden designer and decorator.
She lives in an early Victorian house in Battersea, London.

I CAN STILL remember as a small child the smell of tiny scented tomatoes and damp ferns in my grandfather's greenhouse and it is ever since then that I have dreamed of having a garden room of my own.

The word conservatory conjures up in many people's minds a large space containing one or two different palm trees, masses of ferns and some orchids. Mine is not like that at all. It certainly could never be described as large and it gives you the impression that most of the garden has been brought inside. And yet, among a profusion of flowering plants, this space of only twelve foot by ten serves as my workroom, dining room, greenhouse and potting shed.

The effect I wanted to achieve was that of white brick walls entirely covered with climbing plants and a great mass of foliage and flowers. It has happened all too soon and after a little over a year some of the plants already need cutting back.

One corner of the room is dominated by a huge South African lime *Sparmannia africana*, a Victorian favourite, which has nearly reached the roof, creating a jungle effect with its huge leaves. The exotic white flowers last for months. Few plants bring back memories of the Mediterranean so well as the citrus trees blossoming and fruiting together and smelling delicious. Mine, a *Citrus* × mitis, seems to do this most of the year and as I have had it for ten years it is an old favourite. The tiny oranges which are bitter make very good marmalade. Taking up more than its fair share of space is a datura cutting I took, *D. cornigera* 'Knightii', which has grown five feet in one and a half years. It should have trumpet-shaped double

The conservatory is linked to the backgarden lawn by a York stone path and terrace.

white flowers about eight inches long but as yet they have not appeared. My mother says this is because I purloined the cutting.

When I bought the house two years ago there were the remains of a small dilapidated Victorian conservatory tacked on the back, leading from the sitting room through a french window. I pulled it down and started again. This left a perfect space between my house wall and my neighbour's garden wall and as it seemed so simple I made the design myself and had my builders put it together. I found a pair of conservatory doors from a house also built around 1850, had windows made to match and built a glass roof. There is a wonderful feeling of space now and the conservatory has become an extension of the sitting room and kitchen as well as of the garden.

There are a round table, chairs and a comfortable old wicker chair much appreciated by the neighbour's cat. As there is no staging the plants stand in wire *jardinières*, on low tables and in pots on the floor. It is difficult to believe but there are over eighty terracotta pots of all sizes, including two large nineteenth-century ones with neoclassical figures and another early nineteenth-century blue and white Persian pot. The only other feature is an enormous mirror in a plain white frame on one wall making the room look twice the size. Pinoleum blinds under the roof prevent the plants getting scorched when it is very hot and are essential as the conservatory faces due south. They also make a cosier atmosphere at night. The lighting is a mixture of candles, spotlights and lamps with waterproof switches. There are Mexican terracotta tiles on the floor following through from the kitchen, they are a wonderful colour and are easily cleaned after I have been spraying or re-potting.

Climbing plants are, so to speak, the wallpaper

of a conservatory and unlike the other plants cannot be easily rearranged and so need planning first. I have three different varieties of passion flower. *Passiflora × caeruleo-racemosa*, which has

A place in the sun, part dappled by shade from the leaves of Sparmannia africana. *Past the rattan chair a door opens into the kitchen.*

purplish pink flowers, *P. edulis* with huge leaves and beautiful green and white flowers which I hope will produce some fruit one day, and a pure white one called Constance Elliot. They are all vigorous

and look wonderful entwined around each other flowering together in the summer. A hardier blue one, *P. caerulea*, has found its way in through the open window from the garden to join them.

I have always loved blue flowers and there is hardly a prettier blue than that of plumbago. It is also summer flowering and would probably rather be in a bed, but does not seem to mind a large pot too much providing it is well fed. I rescued two stephanotis grown on dreadful round hoops from a friend who was throwing them away and a year later they have reached the roof, climbed round two walls and have flowered twice. Their glossy evergreen leaves and highly scented white flowers make them a marvellous conservatory plant. Two other evergreen climbers I have are the Chinese jasmine, *Trachelospermum jasminoides*, mine is the variegated one, with jasmine-like white flowers appearing in July and August and smelling very strongly, and the wax flower, *Hoya carnosa*, which I am training on wires across the roof. It has quaint star-like flowers hanging in clusters. The other climber worth a mention is a sinister-looking plant from Tasmania with purple bell-like fruits called *Billardiera longiflora*.

Among the pots which can easily be moved there is a lemon tree, *Citrus limonum*, with large lemons on it, but who knows if they will ever ripen. Also from the Mediterranean are two oleanders in different shades of pink which flower from May until October. They always remind me of auto-routes, although mine are rather special varieties. Piled up on tables in front of the windows are masses of large white petunias, geraniums and various other white plants. They almost fill the window space, spilling out of their containers and trailing to the floor, and the flowers seem to light up at night. I must not forget the three half-dead gardenias I bought for 50 pence each and brought back to life, for they have flowered for the last two months and filled the whole house with their scent. A conservatory is a very good place for reviving ailing plants but the trouble is that I get offered an awful lot of patients.

Pots galore, with one balanced on an antique jardinière, *more on a wrought iron table. Plants include* Lilium regale *and orange trees.*

As the conservatory is a working greenhouse as well as a house extension, ventilation is essential and there are three automatic ventilators in the roof to provide this. The main convector radiator is run off the central heating and can easily be boosted if the conservatory is being used as a dining room in the winter. There is an additional electric fan heater thermostatically controlled which comes on automatically if the temperature drops and the central heating is off. I usually keep it between 40° and 45° F and it is surprising how great a variety of plants, many thought to be tender, can be grown in a comparatively cool house.

The plants must be treated individually as their needs vary and while I think it worthwhile taking extra care with a difficult or unusual one, I would rather grow plants which are suited to their environment. I move all the pots around from time to time so the plants get their fair share of light. Larger plants shade small pots of cuttings and seedlings when they come out of the propagators. In hot weather I have to water most of the plants every day and all the lime haters get rain-water from a butt in the garden. As they dry out very quickly in pots they have to be watched carefully and when I go away I arrange a plant sitter. Nearly everything is sprayed with water at least once a day in hot weather and all the plants get a weekly feed with Phostrogen during the growing season. I am glad to say that during the winter they are not nearly so demanding and I usually only water about once a week. I ought to mention at this point that I grow nearly everything in John Innes composts.

I have only talked about the permanent plants in the conservatory, but there are many more which are moved in and out according to whether or not they are in flower or what the temperature is like outside. Pots of tulips, regale lilies, agapanthus and many others have their turn indoors according to the season. The autumn is a really busy time. All the tender plants which have been put out for the summer, either in the shade among the garden plants or in pots on the terrace, have to be brought in once there is a danger of frost. These include certain azaleas, geraniums, cymbidiums, also a lovely early-flowering *Camellia sasanqua* and a particularly favourite pot of bright blue

Convolvulus sabatius (syn. *C. mauritanicus*). Some of these plants flower in the winter.

The conservatory makes a very agreeable potting shed. I can never resist taking cuttings and collecting seeds wherever I go and spend hours propagating them, consequently few of my plants have actually been bought. Occasionally I get the labels mixed up and recently what I thought was a box of parsley turned out to be tiny acacia trees. One of my cuttings which has been a great success is a perennial morning glory *Ipomoea learii*, the blue dawn flower. The dark royal blue flowers come out in the early morning and gradually fade in the sunlight during the day and by evening are pale mauve. It has already found its way round three walls of the conservatory and has also wormed its way outside through a gap in the window left open for the summer.

In the daytime the table is cleared for work. The conservatory has proved an ideal place for this as the light is so good even on very dreary winter days. As most of my work involves garden design, planting plans for clients and plant research, I find the atmosphere inspiring, although I often look up and notice something which needs doing; a dry plant or a climber waving about looking for something to cling to and I inevitably become waylaid for an hour or two.

At night the same table seats up to eight people. In the summer the front of the conservatory is opened up and the garden is lit so it is rather like sitting outside and although the plants are beginning to crowd the dining area, it is a wonderful place to eat and the atmosphere is always relaxed.

And so to bed – not, as yet, in the conservatory but that too might be a possibility one day.

I certainly feel this is my favourite room in the house and cannot envisage living without one again. I sometimes imagine what it will be like when there is no room for anything or anyone but the plants, and then start dreaming of another one double the size. I would welcome twice as much work but am not sure about sixteen people to dinner.

A view from the Kitchen across to a large mirror. Pinoleum blinds give shade and privacy.

LORD ELIOT

*Lord Eliot is the heir to the Earl of St Germans and lives with
his wife and three sons at Port Eliot, a stately home in Cornwall.*

I DO NOT like change. Life goes on in much the same way here as it has done for a very long time. Some things are added to, some disintegrate and disappear, and others just slowly evolve; it's very peaceful. I have a leisurely way of life, that's how I like it. I have lived here all my life and feel at one with the house and the land.

There are plans of course for improvements at Port because I am at the moment the person continuing the tradition. Some of these plans have been completed; others are in progress, and major decisions are arrived at in an unhurried way. It is incredible to be on the receiving end of thirty generations of one family, for I am the thirtieth Eliot to live here, and I thank them all for affording me the enjoyment of their plans and husbandry.

My main contribution to the grounds is the maze, which was built ten years ago. From the mound in the centre you can stand and look down an avenue of hedges in a straight line over to a distant hill where the sun rises. On this hill I intend to raise a monument indicating the spot where the midwinter solstice occurs. Innovations like these in the grounds where Repton contrived so many delights in the eighteenth century are gestures in the grand manner, but why not? The implications of Capital Transfer Tax are such that one day Port Eliot will be open to the public. I feel that a maze is what future visitors would expect to find at a place like this.

Originally there was a Celtic settlement here, which probably accounts for the mysterious atmosphere you sense at certain times and in certain lights whilst in the garden surrounded by rhododendrons and azaleas, beneath mature oak trees with cathedral-like proportions.

The house stands on the site of a former tenth-century Augustinian monastery, and came into the family's possession on the Dissolution. At that time, the main monastic building included a refectory and a dormitory, together with many secular appendages, including warehouses, a bakery, tannery, pottery, mill and smithy, all part of the ordered self-contained monastic existence. As the Eliot family became more prosperous, mainly through a fortuitous marriage in the eighteenth century to one Hester Booth, a courtesan and dancer, so their tastes developed as they became subject to more up-country influences. Their new wealth afforded them the opportunity of taking these outhouses within the curtilage of their main dwelling.

The conservatory stands on the site of the former dormitory of the Augustinian priory at the extreme eastern end of the house. It is a place you pass through en route to the garden. Since I can remember, the conservatory has almost always been empty. It is an exquisite little room with a delicate vaulted roof, recently replaced and painted terre-verte after extensive deathwatch beetle had been found. The windows still have the original centrifugally spun glass. In earlier days, large panes of glass were made by pouring the molten material on to the centre of a spinning disc. Centrifugal forces then spread the glass over the disc. When this material solidified, there was a 'bull's eye' at the centre. This useless piece of glass was often appropriated by the workmen and set in

Plants including tongue fern, avocado pear, yucca, indoor jasmine, orchid, oleander and spingi are gathered below the trompe-l'oeil *trellis at the east end of the orangery.*

A view of the interior of the orangery with an iron chair which had been in the grounds since the early 19th century; cordyline palm in foreground (OVERLEAF)

the windows of their cottages. It strikes me as odd that today people will actually buy at a premium a contrived bull's eye and place it with pride in their front doors.

The orangery is the principal structure in the garden and a few minutes' walk from the conservatory. It has been attributed to Sir John Soane, but I suspect this is wishful thinking. It stands on the site of some ancient building associated with the monastery. In front of the orangery and to the south there is a small formal garden, surrounded by an ancient yew hedge which had become very misshapen. This has now recovered from a severe cutting back, and is restored to its former precise pattern. It is within this little enclosure that the only herbaceous border occurs, for I believe that there should be a 'dearth of earth' within the pleasure gardens of a place like this.

When I was a child I rarely played in the gardens, which were more or less out of bounds. However, occasionally I was obliged to have tea in the orangery with my grandparents and their friends. Tea included all the Edwardian trimmings of cakes and biscuits, sandwiches and scones with

Beside the oak leaf carved wood table in the conservatory, a collection of plaques for tree planting date from the early nineteenth Century. One inscription reads 'Abies morinda planted by The Marchioness, Cornwallis 1850 Himalayas'.

quince jam and Cornish cream. On these occasions my grandfather, venerable with age and a trifle senile, would often ask me who I was. 'Who are you?' he would say. 'I am Peregrine, grandpapa.' 'Hmm, what a funny name,' he would mutter as he

Close-up of Eltex greenhouse heater dating from 1920s.

pottered off, wondering whether I was his brother, his son or a contemporary of his from school. I recall the orangery then as a strangely eerie place, with an air of other-worldliness. During the next thirty years, the orangery slowly decayed nearly to the point of no return, until finally I embarked on a plan involving its total restoration. It has been reroofed with random-hung Delabole slates, and the entire south-facing glass wall has been repaired, although little actual renewal had to take place because the materials with which the fenestration had been constructed were of the soundest pitch-pine. The slated floor of the building was all higgledy-piggledy, with uneven slabs rising from the undulations of the collapsing heating system. The extremely ingenious arrangement of flues running to and fro beneath this floor has been levelled and moth-balled. The square floor slates were relaid on the diagonal, as opposed to the square, which I think is richer to the eye. The trellis work which my grandfather designed and put here in the twenties was dismantled, reassembled and repainted in the lightest shade of terre-verte. When it comes to decorating trellis work, it is important that the strongest tone created should be the shadow cast upon the wall by the trellis itself. People often make the mistake of decorating their trellises in too dark a colour, and spoil this subtlety. The last remaining item to complete the restoration of the orangery is to reconstitute the little formal fountains found both in the building and its adjacent enclosure. The statuary in the orangery was mostly brought back at the time when the Grand Tour was part of a young Englishman's education, shipped from Italy direct to the quays at Port Eliot. I would like to place some of these statues in the gardens, but this can't be done owing to their extreme age and the likely damage that would be caused during the winter. However, as and when large trees need felling in the gardens, I usually have them cut, leaving six to eight foot stumps. These are then carved into fanciful shapes and covered with old lead roofing sheet, recycled from the valleys and gutters of the house.

The rest of the garden comprises some forty or fifty acres, and can best be described as a woodland garden. There are many drives around the plantation on which to walk. Off these drives are smaller paths which lead you through vast laurel hedges into enclosures where you will find collections of plants. These clearings can be considered separate individual gardens within the plantation. There is, for instance, a rhododendron garden, one containing camellias, another exclusively planted with azaleas; there is a bowling green. Similarly, the maze is in its own space, concealed from general view. In each of these clearings are to be found summerhouses, statues, ponds or terraces.

One of the most pleasing walks in the plantation is along the banks of the St Germans estuary, on which there is a lovely thatched boathouse. A principal feature of this walk, apart from the beauties of nature, is a hugely tall and elegant railway viaduct designed by Isambard Kingdom Brunel, one of many to be found on the Great Western Railway. Immediately beneath this viaduct is a 'Fanciful Fortification', housing a collection of eighteenth-century French naval guns. These were bought by my family shortly after Trafalgar, the money raised going for comforts to the wounded.

The gardens do not form part of the view from the house, which is built on a steep north-facing hillside, always the mark of a Celtic settlement. From ancient times until the eighteenth century, the area in front of the house was a tidal basin. Humphry Repton was commissioned to transform this into a park. By diverting the river with a low dam and filling in the basin with waste material brought from Plymouth, where the Georgian docks were being constructed, he was able to raise the level above the tide. A lot of infill was also taken from a quarry on the opposite side of the tidal basin. When enough material had been taken, the whole quarry was turned into an elaborate nightmare, with low-relief carvings of fanciful buildings, caves, tunnels, grottoes, etc. People in the village say the place is haunted, but I am uncertain this is so.

My memories of living here are all happy ones. It is my fairyland. For me, Port Eliot is where the rainbow ends.

Lord Eliot and his dog seated in the conservatory below a Habsburg gothick lantern.

INDEX

Numbers in *italics* refer to illustrations